Kinaesthesia in the Psychology, Philosophy and Culture of Human Experience

This accessible book explores the nature and importance of kinaesthesia, considering how action, agency and movement intertwine and are fundamental in feeling embodied in the world.

Bringing together psychological, philosophical and cultural perspectives, the book examines the subjective feeling of movement in a cross-disciplinary manner. It discusses kinaesthesia through the framework of embodied cognition and outlines how contemporary discussion in psychology and phenomenology can inform our understanding of everyday experience. The book also sketches a framework for full appreciation of the sense of movement in performance and cultural life, discussing how a sense of movement is central to one's agency. It is composed in four 'movements', aiming to achieve a connected and original argument for why movement matters, an argument exemplified in dance. The first movement explains the science of kinaesthesia and the history of the concept, the second quiet movement reflects on the psychological and philosophical dimensions of the sense of movement and links it to a discussion of current thought informed by phenomenology and embodied cognition, the third movement turns to the culture of movement in dance and walking, and the fourth rests with the pleasures of movement, and emphasizes the social dimensions of movement in gesture and agency.

This wide-ranging book is a must read for all those interested in the psychology of movement, embodied cognition, performance studies and the interaction between psychology and dance. It will also be of interest to students and practitioners of embodied movement and dance practice therapies.

Roger Smith is Emeritus Reader in History of Science at Lancaster University, UK.

Kinaesthesia in the Psychology, Philosophy and Culture of Human Experience

Roger Smith

LONDON AND NEW YORK

First published 2023
by Routledge
4 Park Square, Milton Park, Abingdon, Oxon OX14 4RN

and by Routledge
605 Third Avenue, New York, NY 10158

Routledge is an imprint of the Taylor & Francis Group, an informa business

British Library Cataloguing-in-Publication Data
A catalogue record for this book is available from the British Library

ISBN: 978-1-032-43590-9 (hbk)
ISBN: 978-1-032-43588-6 (pbk)
ISBN: 978-1-003-36802-1 (ebk)

DOI: 10.4324/9781003368021

Typeset in Times New Roman
by MPS Limited, Dehradun

Contents

PART IV
Fourth movement: allegro 107

Illustrations

Preface

Moving, people feel alive; and if an animal or person is alive, we expect it to move, even in a minimal way. The feeling of movement is elemental. Yet it has many components and presents many challenges for description and understanding. This short book about kinaesthesia introduces different perspectives on awareness of posture and movement based on sensation from muscles and joints in the body. These perspectives belong to different disciplines. The book aims to relate different fields, and thus achieve a wide view, rather than to contribute detail to any one field.

I came to the topic of movement through intellectual history and history of science, and as a result I first documented the history of the notion of kinaesthesia, a history which focused on the association of touch and movement with the human feel for reality. I published *The Sense of Movement: An Intellectual History* (London, Process Press, 2019). The present book is different. Writing from psychological, philosophical and cultural perspectives on human experience, I emphasize and explain the importance of kinaesthesia in embodied life and in the scientific, artistic and everyday culture in which it is embedded. I draw on the earlier work, but I do not again go over the history. The very basic place of kinaesthetic awareness has often not been appreciated. The present book seeks to rectify this.

Biological and psychological approaches to experienced self-movement and posture give a central place to notions of kinaesthesia, proprioception and haptic sense. These notions will be made clear. The main purpose of the book, however, is to relate these notions and the science of which they are part to philosophical and cultural interests. It is necessary to be informed about science and specialist debate within the academic disciplines 'touching on' awareness of self-movement. But it is not my part to contribute to the technical side of science or philosophy; for this, there are many specialists and a large literature to match. I start, rather, with the fact that everyone has at least some tacit or implicit knowledge of felt movement, and I build on that in order to relate felt movement to the interests of the humanities, the social sciences, therapeutic practices, the daily world of walking and the performance arts, especially dance. Understanding the ways in which scientific biology and psychology relate to everyday activity, common intuitions and the surrounding culture is as much part of objective knowledge as the content of science.

In modest ways, I am also a mover, and to a degree I keep the personally and historically informed voice rather than writing like a professional psychologist or philosopher. The book, therefore, may speak more naturally to readers with interests in the humanities. Yet, I hope that psychologists and philosophers and their students with broad interests, and certainly the wider audience interested in psychology and philosophy, will welcome these perspectives on kinaesthesia informed by contemporary culture. I write especially with readers who move in mind, move perhaps in dance or physical theatre, perhaps in embodied therapies, perhaps in sports or walking, but certainly in everyday life. As everyone moves, it might be said that the book is for everyone.

The book lightly plays with classical musical form and is divided into 'movements'. I acknowledge quotations and sources, but there are no footnotes. The list of references picks out a number of accessible sources. I eschew jargon, and where it is much used in relevant literature, I explain it. I italicize key terms on their first appearance. I put apostrophes, or scare-quotes, around certain words or phrases in order to draw attention to where I 'touch on' relevant metaphorical or figurative content; sensitivity to this content reveals the depth and pervasiveness of reference to felt movement in language and culture.

I published the historical book, *The Sense of Movement*, with the press founded by the late Bob Young (Robert M. Young), with whom I shared the thinking behind my work. Em Farrell now manages Process Press, and I warmly thank her for support and for permission to draw on this work. A number of psychologists, including James Good, Hroar Klempe, Graham Richards, Wade Pickren and members of the Society for the History of Psychology, Division 26 of the American Psychological Association, persuaded me to interact more directly with their (vast and diverse) discipline, and especially to take on board research on embodied cognition. My colleague in the history of science, Daniel Todes, pressed me and offered support in thinking further about the relation between the academic and the personal voice. His encouragement and critical thought has mattered. Anonymous readers for Routledge certainly helped with their criticisms. Tomasz

Jaworski brought a much valued professional eye to help with the illustrations and I am very grateful. At Routledge, I thank Emilie Coin, a psychology editor, for her breadth of interest in taking on this book, and I thank her and Khyati Sanger for professional support.

For over twenty years, before the catastrophe of the war in the Ukraine, I lived in Moscow, Russia, with friends who, amongst other things, are psychologists, historians, therapists, philosophers, literary scholars or artists, and their concerns are reflected here. My brother-in-law, Sergei, marvellously upheld my electronic connections. In response to the COVID-19 pandemic, I became interested in the difference that physical presence makes to human relations, and in this context I thank the Editorial Board of *Consortium Psychiatricum*, an innovative Moscow psychiatry journal, for encouraging me to publish my comments (vol. 1/2, 2020 and vol. 3/2, 2022) and to develop them further here. I am also grateful to the Institute of Philosophy of the Russian Academy of Sciences in Moscow for granting me an honorary position and for publishing my work in its journal, *Философский журнал/The Philosophy Journal*. I participated with vivacious people in studios of musical movement led by Aida Ailamazyan and by Tatiana Trifonova. Cooperation between Moscow's Research University, the Higher School of Economics, and Goldsmiths, University of London, thanks to the jointly brilliant Liudmila Alyabieva and Anna Furse, created PeARL (Performance and Artistic Research Laboratory) and fostered collaboration which made me think much more closely about movement and performance. I thank Natasha Fedunina and Danya for 'moving' company and Ruth O'Dowd for her embodied thoughts. In this world, and through many warm reflections on it with Irina Sirotkina and through her generous knowledge of movement culture, and through her movement, I began to explore with people why I think movement matters. This book is the result.

With sorrow and joy I dedicate the book to all my Russian colleagues and friends.

Roger Smith
Durham, England, November 2022

Part I

First movement: theme and variations

1   Being alive

Children or adults stare at an insect, a worm, an animal or a human body. Perhaps there is a heap of matted fur lying in the road or perhaps someone has fainted. Asking whether the beast or body is alive, witnesses search for a slight movement? Children poke an animal to see. Adults feel for the pulse or look for breathing. Is there life?

Is it moving?

Curiosity and feeling link movement and signs of life. When the sculptor Pygmalion carved a statue and created his ideal of a beautiful woman in marble, it was her movement which first made him see that she, astoundingly, had come alive.

Visible or tangible movement in the human animal is the outward sign of an inner force. Death cuts movement short.

Humans move, and they know that they move, and when they move, the feelings and intuitions they have for movement have a very large place in self-awareness of being alive (Fingerhut and Marienberg 2012). Much of the time this awareness is ill-defined and rather bland, even unnoticed; the feelings involved seem to be part of a general consciousness that being alive is being with a body embedded in a physical world – animals are *embodied*. The human animal's knowledge of this is profoundly bound up with moving. And through embodied movement everyone is *in relations* with the surroundings, the world of people, physical things and the environment (Smith 2020, 2022). This is the life-world (the term introduced by phenomenologists) or the *Umwelt* (the biological term introduced by Jakob von Uexküll, literally translated as the surrounding world), both terms embedding the organism, or person, in the immediate world that has meaning for the organism's, or person's, life. In the words of Gabriel Josipovici, 'we are embodied, and it is our bodies which give us common access to the physical world; in other words, we are participants, not spectators' (Josipovici 1996, p. 6).

DOI: 10.4324/9781003368021-2

Figure 1.1 Honoré Daumier. Pygmalion, from Histoire ancienne series, *Le Charivari*, 28 December 1842. Lithograph. In the public domain.

This book is about the world of living movement known by *participation* and about the awareness, or feel, of movement that goes with it. I ask *why movement matters*. To this end, I lay out for discussion different aspects of the human experience of kinaesthesia, the sensory accompaniment of the position and change of position of the body and tension in muscles and joints.

Experience of movement is boundless in its variety. I joyfully recall walking in the Geghama mountain range of central Armenia. Though

Figure 1.2 Samvel Manukian walking in the Geghama Mountains, Armenia, August 2021. Photograph, Irina Sirotkina. In the author's collection.

the tops are at well over 3,000 meters, it is walking not climbing country: the mountains are long extinct volcanoes, and a number retain smooth conical form and have lake-filled craters, beautiful, like eyes. Walking across the grass covered and rock strewn slopes, there are continuously changing relations between my movement and the landscape.

I was not 'looking at' but 'being in' – intensely alive. Something very deep-lying and intuitive links sensed movement to the feeling of being alive.

It is important to understand that maintaining a posture, including 'resting', involves the same processes and the same kinds of conscious perceptions, the same kinaesthetic sensations, as movement. Posture and movement are both activities, and posture involves activity comparable with and dependent on the same functional system in the body as the activity needed for movement and balance. 'Stillness demands precise adaptation to the micro-movements of a shifting equilibrium. To stand still you have to move' (E. Manning 2009, p. 43). When this book refers to movement, the implied contrast is therefore not with rest but with death.

The book is about the life of sensed or felt movement (and posture). Why do children and animals so evidently run for pleasure, or a terrified person 'freeze' with fear? Why dance crazes? Why might a sedentary author long to move on foot through a mountain landscape? The discussion of questions like these leads into a startlingly wide range of really rather basic issues about the way to describe and explain the human place in the world.

It is absolutely central to thinking about the feel of movement 'to grasp' that *movement encounters resistance*. The resistance may come from the body, from the natural world, from other people, from institutions, from anything. But it is there, and the 'thereness' of resistance is logically and materially basic to awareness that there is an action.

A person moving is aware of activity, and at the same time is aware that something, perhaps the body, perhaps someone or perhaps a physical object resists the activity; perhaps this resistance even moves the person. There is consciousness of what it is possible and not possible to do by acting, by exercising a force. The relations of forces, the balance and conflict of forces, between an acting self and a resisting not-self enacts a life. This life has a subjective character, in which connection there is talk about the psychological world, and an objective character, in which connection there is talk about the biological body, about the natural and social worlds and about all the forces or powers which they exercise. Discussing the feel of movement immerses self-understanding in an ocean of issues in thought and practice about how mind and body relate and about how subjective and objective worlds connect.

Consider the outward movement of the limbs in standing up and the inward consciousness that goes with standing. There is evidently a relationship between the fact of movement and the consciousness of movement. But what is it? The body, through kinaesthetic sensation, informs the mind, since it tells the mind that standing is happening. (The philosophical psychologist Shaun Gallagher wrote a book with the title, *How the Body Shapes the Mind*; Gallagher 2005.) It is also the case that the mind informs the body, since the body customarily stands up when a person decides it should. There is, however, another way to describe what is going on, a way which does not use language treating mind and body as if they were concrete and separate entities. This alternative describes persons, not minds or bodies, as *actors* or *agents*. It employs a *language of movement* bringing about change and questions reference to an 'inner', mental or subjective world and an 'outer', physical or objective world. It suggests that it is a matter of convention, however deeply established, to divide processes into inner and outer, mental and physical. For example, imagine a pilgrimage and try to draw the line between the inner experience and the outer walk. In order to understand the movement taking place and experienced, it is necessary to know about the sort of activity in which the pilgrim is participating. For sure, to take another illustration, in vision we 'look out on' (and a person has an 'outlook'). All the same, vision is also an activity, both in the narrow sense that it involves movement of the eyeballs and in the wider sense that all perception is an active engagement with rather than passive reception of the world.

Moving, a person faces questions about what kind of force and how much force it is possible, as an individual or collectively, to exercise. How far and in what way do forces originate within the individual and how far is a person moved by forces originating without in bodies, nature, institutions, tradition or government? The whole issue of the respect and concern due to individual people and to groups of people, to their power and freedom, cannot be decided independently of knowledge of the balance between action and resistance and of con-sciousness of that balance. At stake is *agency*: where does the power to bring something about, the power 'to make a move', lie? In movement, or in attempting to move, or even in just staying as one is, everyone knows something about power and resistance. The last part of the book therefore 'turns' from the feel of movement to the question of agency. The global tragedy of migrants, or of huge prison populations or, more mundanely, the daily round of work is accompanied by awareness of power to move and power to stop movement. Subjective feelings accompany the balance of these powers: felt movement, or resistance to it, is not emotionally neutral. Awareness of the distri-bution of power to move shapes the subjective identity of those who move and those who do not. These feelings have a large place in the very notions of self and self-worth.

Human possibilities and capacities for movement manifestly vary very widely – from the marathon runner to those people with conditions where mobility is the big issue. Outside coma, cases in which almost no movement is possible are rare, and even in coma the movements of the lungs and heart persist. There is, though, a rare condition in which kinaesthesia is almost totally lost, and the consequences are colossal.

Talk about people's awareness of their own movement is talk about something very fundamental to being human. Yet, at first glance paradoxically, for the most part in everyday life there is little thought about or reflection on the sense of movement. One result, as we shall see, is that writers use the word kinaesthesia very loosely. Human animals walk, dance, balance, tap fingers on a keyboard, move mouth and throat and lungs and speak, gesture, move a foot to a rhythm. They just do these things without much thought. Even when there is a plan to move, often enough there is little or no thought about the component movements needed and little reflection, unless something goes very well or very wrong, as they take place. There is normally no consciousness of the movements of breathing or the heart-beat. William James took for granted the continuous presence of bodily awareness and linked it to movement, yet he passed on without mentioning kinaesthesia:

> The nucleus of every man's experience, the sense of his own body, is ... an absolutely continuous perception; and equally continuous is his perception (though it may be very inattentive) of a material environment of that body, changing by gradual transition when the body moves. (James 2000, p. 235)

Nevertheless, even though they may not pay much attention, people generally know when they are moving and that they are alive. In especially happy, difficult or fearful moments, or in conditions of illness, this awareness is vivid and a person may exclaim about feeling 'fully alive' or 'half-dead'.

It is as well to make clear early on what can and cannot be accomplished in a wide-ranging but short book. The book is about awareness of self-movement and the place of kinaesthesia is this awareness; it is not about perception of movement in the surrounding world. (There is, for instance, no discussion of film.) This may be thought a somewhat problematic decision, since the psychological facts indicate that the perception of self-movement and the perception of movement in surrounding people or things are intimately linked. At times in talk about a person's moving body, it is not clear whether the talk is about movement of self or of something other. For example, persons who experience epileptic convulsions may feel that their bodies' movements are not theirs. In the light of such considerations, there can be no strict and fast line separating different types of movement perception. But there has been a vast amount of scientific research on perceptual processes, including perception of movement in objects, and it would require a different book to go into this. Much less has been written about the feel of kinaesthesia, not least because it is always present and much harder to shape as the object of experimental inquiry. There is good reason to make this the focus of attention.

The book similarly and in a related way does not attend to weight perception in objects, awareness of the body's own weight and the sense of balance. Consciousness of weight and balance are certainly fundamental to the sense of movement, as any climber, dancer or gymnast will confirm. The fact is, human senses of the body and what it is doing are very complex indeed, and any way of picturing part of this complexity will involve simplification. I shall simplify by leaving questions about weight and balance for another time. There is, once again, reason to get at least a large part of the picture straight, the picture of kinaesthesia.

Further, it is common for psychologists to talk about people in general, as if there were some kind of universal norm of human nature to which they have specialist access. This book began in the same vein, linking the feel of movement to the feel of life. Yet, talk in this way goes only so far and, indeed, may quickly become invidious. People, both individually and as members of the groups with which they identify (by ethnicity, gender, age, nationality, etc.), are enormously variable. It appears to be true, for example, that sensitivity to movement varies considerably from person to person. Observers of dance report very varied responses and many factors are involved (Reason and Reynolds 2010). Some people report that they empathize with the dancers' movements; but I, for one, at least consciously, hardly do that. The bare-foot tracker does not feel the ground in the same way as a boot-shod hiker (Ingold 2004).

There is plentiful historical and ethnographic evidence for the extraordinary range and variety of human belief and practices. So much is this so, that as Geoffrey Lloyd commented,

> in both history and ethnography we have severe hermeneutic problems in coming to terms with how the world has been understood, to the point where the question has been raised whether indeed it is the same world that is being understood. (Lloyd 2012, p. 2)

An obvious limitation of the present discussion is, therefore, the absence of comparative data about what movement means in different cultures. We know, for example, that feeling the pulse played an important part in ancient Greek medicine, as it did and does in Chinese medicine (Kuriyama 1999). Chinese culture, for instance, has the concept of *Qi*, which, loosely understood, brings about activity in general and is life-force in particular, of which movement is the visible sign. Pacific cultures have the notion of *mana*, while numerous writers in English have referred to 'the dance of life'. Nevertheless, there is little knowledge about any differences that may exist in the feel of movement and kinaesthetic awareness among different groups of people, let alone comparison of notions of being, reality and agency that may relate to this sensibility. Some studies of the changes the modern world has brought about to the feeling of movement are an exception (Schwartz 1992).

The comparative anthropology of dance suggests itself as a possible route of inquiry. Comparative questions, however, pose a conundrum: we must presuppose that other people share something in common for us to communicate with them at all; yet, we also want to recognize difference. Comparative psychological studies of sensations exist (classically, they concern colour perception) but arriving at agreed results, results that would settle argument about the existence of human universals, has not (perhaps yet) proved possible (Bender and Beller 2016).

The book is about the ideas and expression of felt movement in contemporary Western culture and is not a scientific monograph. Awareness of movement has a history, though as I have written about the history at length elsewhere, I do not here go into detail (Smith 2019a). The book sets out to be sensitive to philosophical questions, but it does not claim to resolve points in philosophy. It makes a large claim about the contribution of the sense of movement to what the authors discussed say about reality; this, however, is not the same as making a claim about what reality really is. The literature in philosophy for and against realism is huge, views diverge and even those who do hold it is possible to make statements about reality differ over what they say about the nature of reality. This book is concerned with the large and impressive body of thought which states that the sense of movement, often subsumed under the sense of touch, is the means by which people (implicitly all people) most directly encounter the reality of the physical world and hence know themselves as embodied actors in the world.

The book also addresses aspects of the mind-body relation, not so much as a philosophical problem but as an intrinsic part of human life. Building on the way the language of movement and felt movement offers descriptive alternatives to the language of the interaction of bodily (or neural) mechanisms and mental states and functions, I reach a conclusion with a philosophical dimension. Explaining this requires some informal appreciation of phenomenology, the endeavour to characterize the conscious world ('the phenomena') as it presents itself, without presuppositions and while suspending beliefs about the derivation of this world from some other supposed reality (such as nature, or society or a deity). There is room for a closer descriptive analysis of the place of kinaesthesia in the conscious world. Happily, there is a large and dynamic domain of research in contemporary psychology, under the umbrella of embodied cognition, which, in conjunction with methods taken from phenomenology, is taking this up (Gallagher 2017; Gallagher and Zahavi 2021). I discuss this in the second part of the book.

Commonly enough, everyday English calls psychology the science of mind and physiology the science of body. It is usage fraught with difficulty, and not just with the obvious problem of saying how mind and body, and hence also psychology and physiology as areas of research, relate. There is something wrong about the adoption of mind and body as fundamental categories of the understanding. (A category, in this usage, is a class of things or assertions which are taken to be fundamental in the world.) One clear sign of this is the difficulty of translating the word mind into other languages. In Russian, for example, there is no one word for mind: '*um*' is the closest, but more precisely translated as wits; '*razum*' is reason or intellect; '*soznaniye*' is consciousness or recognition; and the mental functions, like memory, are individually specified. (Is it the case, then, that Russian speakers, not having the word mind, have no minds?) A further sign is that, in practice, body and mind work in tandem. As Laurence Sterne wrote: 'A Man's body and his mind, with the utmost reverence to both I speak it, are exactly like a jerkin, and a jerkin's lining – rumple the one – you rumple the other' (Sterne 1967, p. 174). 'Rumple' is one of many words denoting motion, which Sterne rendered as the shared folding of the outer and inner sides of a jacket. Surely enough, body and mind 'rumple' together, just as they also often work at odds with each other, as when excess passion makes someone awkward. In fact, there is talk about body and mind acting together or acting at odds because such talk expresses the life of a person. The category of *the living person* is more fundamental. The person is 'the ground' in relation to which the mind and body are connected. There are fertile ways to talk about human nature in terms of *life*, or doings, rather than in terms of mind and body, supported by the insight that *all life is movement*. I discuss what people (whole persons, that is, not bodies, or brains or minds) *do,* like dancing and walking. I am far from being alone in inquiring along such lines. Evan Thompson, for instance, systematically elaborated the argument, and the science linking biology and phenomenology through the category of life, establishing continuity between the analysis of mind and analysis of the natural world (Thompson 2007). Considering the more limited case of human life, the social anthropologist Tim Ingold wrote: 'To inquire into human life is thus to explore the conditions of possibility in a world peopled by beings whose identities are established, in the first place, not by received species- or culture-specific attributes but productive accomplishment' (Ingold 2011, p. 7). There is also a mine of relevant, rigorous and precise detail in the arguments and facts of the science of embodied cognition which psychologists and philosophers like Gallagher promote.

Human movement, and also awareness of movement, is always in some way social in character. Becoming a hermit or an island castaway involves taking on a way of life defined by the society to which a person belongs, even as the step is taken to live outside society. Talk about subjective awareness of movement is talk about the subjectivity of an individual person; but it is also talk about the forms of expression and habits of a person who, as a member of a group, has acquired beliefs about the meaning of movement. The dancer, even when dancing solo, does not just move but *performs* as a social act. Performing with others, a dancer creates new kinds of social relations. Performance has subjective and objective dimensions. In a capacious sense, then, the book's topic is *the culture* of movement.

Reference to the social and performative dimensions of movement, and of the feel for movement, opens a perspective on the richness of the English language on movement and the closely related language on touching. (I believe this is true for other languages, but to what extent I must leave it for others to say.) The language is replete with figures of speech about touch and movement commonly, if not always accurately, called metaphors: 'get moving!'; 'a moving appeal'; 'I grasp your point'; 'joining a political movement'; 'the dance of life'; 'the symphony's second movement'; 'she won't move'; 'the movers and shakers of opinion'; 'taking a stance'; 'a clever move'; 'the moving spirit'; 'an uprising'; 'he pointed the way'; 'she took a step up'; 'getting along'; 'get a grip'; 'I was taken for a ride'; and so on. Reference to metaphor derived from sensations originating in the sense organs of the physical body may not be sufficient to understand what is happening here. References to sensed movement are references *to relations, to participation and engagement,* to place and to change of place, and these relations always have a social dimension. One might hear, for instance, 'Speed up!', or, conversely, 'Slow down!' Without context a listener does not know whether this is a command or a piece of advice to a person dawdling in their mind, or to a person walking slowly, or to a person in a panic or to a person running for a train. There was, and is, more to the sense of movement than physiology. If metaphor is involved, what is a metaphor of what – slowness or speed in mind or in body? In the light of modern science, it is common to attribute metaphors to roots in physical sensations, but this may be neither straightforwardly correct nor culturally universal (Lakoff and Johnson 2003).

The seventeenth-century Jansenist philosopher Blaise Pascal wrote: 'Our nature consists in movement; absolute rest is death' (Pascal 1995, §641). His words referred to a spiritual demand in human nature, a requirement to maintain the soul's striving to receive God's grace, and not to a physical movement. The movement at stake was movement in the relation of a person's soul to God. In cultures which take a god or gods to be indisputably real, spiritual reality may be the source of metaphor for material events. Jacques Derrida gave an example from the writing of St John of the Cross, an influential Catholic priest of the Counter-Reformation, in which the flame of the spirit was the source for metaphorical reference to visible flame (Derrida 2005, pp. 247–254). Such examples point to the great range of figures of speech and suggest that talk about metaphor may not be the best way to compare one thing with another. Lloyd, indeed, has recommended talk instead about 'semantic stretch' (Lloyd 2021, pp. 129–130). However this may be decided, the striking fact remains that words invoking movement, and also touch, have an enormously significant place in expression. The language itself signals the importance of felt movement in human life.

The book opened with a picture of movement as the sign of life. This suggests where to look 'to grasp' the significance of movement language: it is living, or life, not the body which may be the source of movement figures of speech. Making this claim, though, it is necessary to confront the fact that biologists in the last two centuries have explained life as the workings of chemical and physical processes, and, in so doing, they appear to have diminished or even eliminated the standing of life as a special or basic category. Indeed, new knowledge and technology has opened life up to manipulation and even made possible the creation of new life-forms. This consideration might imply that the notion of life is simply unavailable to serve as a basic category; it is, rather, physical-chemical mechanism that is basic. Yet, I will argue that it is of considerable importance to relate kinaesthesia and the sense of life (the sense of being alive). The contemporary 'turn' in psychology towards the analysis of action as the basic framework for research, rather than mind or brain, as well as a long history of inquiry into life, supports this 'direction of argument'. We may take life seriously as a category. Most importantly, ordinary speech does so.

This leaves for the introduction a summary of the structure of the book. Playing with the notion of movement, the book has four 'movements', as in many pieces of classical music. A movement refers to 'the manner in which a piece of music "moves"' (*OED* 2007, p. 1867). The term originated with Renaissance dance music, when short pieces accompanied different forms of dance, such as the gigue, and were therefore analogously called movements. Subsequently, usage spread to describe the different parts of other musical forms, such as the symphony. Modern usage also associates different kinds of musical movements with their capacity 'to move' the emotions in different ways.

Within the form given by four movements, the book has twelve chapters. Each is relatively short and deals with a specific topic. The intention is not to provide detail on any particular aspect of awareness of movement but to show how the different aspects relate to each other.

This piece has opened with and then developed the theme – kinaesthesia and the feeling of being alive. The next chapter describes the sense of movement more closely. There are a number of key words and ideas, most especially kinaesthesia and proprioception, to explain. This leads into a history of how kinaesthesia became a subject of inquiry and acquired a place in artistic, philosophical and scientific work.

The second part of the composition is more philosophical and psychological; it is a slow movement. It opens with an account of the importance of felt movement to the sense of reality. This focuses on action encountering resistance. Action-resistance exists as a couple in conscious awareness, as a pair in which the content and meaning of each term depends on contrast or opposition. There is a history of description of this couple as the key to understanding reality: the feel for the real is very much bound up with the touch, movement and bodily senses. The discussion leads into recent psychological argument, informed by phenomenology, under the broad heading of embodied cognition, which is concerned with the life of the acting person (rather than in the first place mind or brain). The discussion also draws in a very different form of psychology, Kleinian psychoanalysis and object relations approaches to the earliest moments of birth. Reality, however it is thought about, is, after all, a matter of birth and death. The chapters in this part of the book explore the very notion of 'contact' or coming together in touch, in the way ordinary language talks about the presence and activity of selves, or persons, in a real world.

As the book was first drafted during a pandemic, the ending of which was repeatedly deferred and which resulted in restrictions and regulations on movement, it includes a brief discussion of the difference between online and offline contact, between digital and face to face encounter and between movement that is only visible and movement involving bodily presence. In the background are questions about the more general impact of digital forms of human relations.

What are the differences between being physically present, in the same space if not literally in touch, with others and communicating digitally? Do these differences matter, and if so, why? What is the difference between recorded and live performance? The last chapter of the movement rounds out this discussion with an introduction to the importance of felt movement to the sense of time. Movement is in time as well as in space.

The book's third movement seeks to dance. That is, it takes up some of the boundless ways, most obviously in dance (though another writer might select sport), in which movement features in cultural life. Dance, as the art form which works with movement and the feelings of both mover and observer of movement, is at the centre of the discussion. Many writers have said that dance is ubiquitous in human existence – past and present. If it is, why? What does knowledge of kinaesthesia bring to reflection on dance? There is a large world of dance studies, and also of dance therapy, that has much to say about this, while participation in a modest way in a form of dance significantly called 'musical movement' informs my own comments. A vast array of other social activities, notably sports, but also such activities as physical theatre and the circus, 'hinge' on movement. I take as a case study the everyday activity of walking. It helps 'move on' the discussion to the key notion of participation. People walk *in* or *with* surroundings; 'in' or 'with' describe the quality of the relations people have with the environment in which they live, whether with landscape (or cityscape), or other people or their own clothed and unclothed bodies.

A musical finale is customarily lively. Here the final movement has three parts, the first concerned with *gesture* and the second with *agency*. Any human movement, and also posture and rest, is a social performance, and as such it can be read as gesture, an embodied form of communication. Thus, the finale takes up the social nature of movement and the social nature of awareness of movement. Walking – and even more obviously running, climbing, dancing or acrobatics – exemplifies the play of the couple of activity-resistance and the relationship of forces or powers. A person's sense of identity and of worth, individually or as a member of a group, has much to do with where the balance of active and resistant forces lies. This is the issue of agency. There is a social attribution of meaning to movement, making movement a form of communication, and there is a social attribution of power to a person, or to a group to which people belong, in opposition to other powers. These are things dancers and other performers, and people in sports, know a lot about, implicitly if not explicitly. They are also things that people in general know about in relation to their own bodies, in families, at work, in the environment and through political participation, again implicitly if not explicitly. Questions of gesture and agency are inseparably bound up with the actualities of being in relations of movement and resistance. The outcome is, indeed, 'the dance of life'. That dance comes to an end with death. But 'along the way', we all move, *con brio*, and it is with the pleasures of movement that the book concludes. The finale, in this vein, tries out the reasoning and feel of what it would be to understand movement as 'ensouled'.

Kinaesthesia may be a feature of being alive which ordinarily receives little attention. Yet, there is a lot to say. As a theme, it 'runs' deep and 'flows' wide.

2 What is the sense of movement?

When you move, you know that you move, and even when you stand, sit or lie still, you know the stillness and where, say, your limbs or backside are. Much of the time, this knowledge is unremarked. Clear self-awareness of movement and posture merges into vague feeling and vague feeling merges into absence of consciousness. As conscious awareness of movement and posture is so variable in degree, and as it seems that actual awareness is of secondary importance in achieving movement and posture, ordinary language often describes the body, muscles or limbs, not the conscious person, 'knowing' what they are doing. There may be reference to the wisdom of the body or to bodily intelligence, even though a stricter use of language would insist that only a person (not a brain or a body) can have wisdom or intelligence. I watched the delicate fingers of an accordion player. He did not look at the fingers, but 'they knew' exactly where they were on the keys, and they skipped or jumped accurately from one key to another, exhibiting refined bodily knowledge.

Persuaded by such experience, it is commonplace to aver that muscles, rather than minds, 'know' best what to do in order to achieve skilful movements like throwing darts at the bull's eye.

There is a considerable research literature about motor skills, about the structural and functional mechanisms in the body (the brain, muscles, joints, tendons, skin and nervous connections of all these organs or tissues). No one doubts the essential place of these mechanisms in human lives (and naturally in the lives of animals too) and their fabulous complexity and subtlety. There are also considerable medical and commercial implications in prosthetics and robotics building on models of these mechanisms. The sheer scale of the refinement of control is obvious. Even an apparently mundane repeated movement, like walking or hitting a nail on the head with a hammer, will be slightly different on each occasion.

DOI: 10.4324/9781003368021-3

Figure 2.1 Accordionist (2006). Photograph, Tomasz Jaworski. Courtesy of Tomasz Jaworski. Copyright © Tomasz Jaworski.

The neuropsychologist A. R. Luria was so impressed by the art of movement sequences in achieving motility that he referred to the body's 'kinetic melody' (Luria 1973, p. 32; Sheets-Johnstone 2012, pp. 47–51).

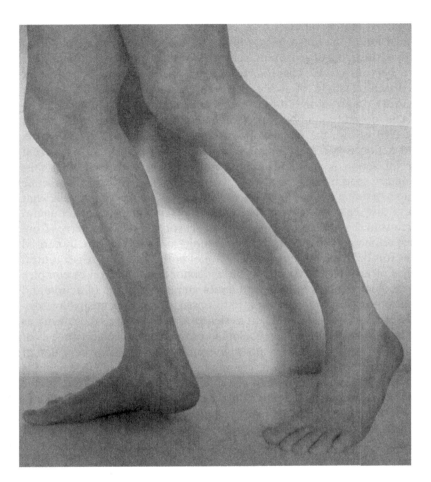

Figure 2.2 Moving legs. Photograph, Irina Sirotkina. In the author's collection.

Much scientific research focuses on the mechanisms in the body which serve to maintain posture and to make motility possible, and at the same time, sometimes but certainly not always, give rise to awareness of posture, balance and movement, awareness that runs from a sharply delineated consciousness to the dimmest of perceptions. Research encompasses both work that stresses the periphery of the body, the organs of movement, and work that stresses the centre, the brain. The first approach focuses on the sensory endings in muscles, joints and other tissues that send information, as nervous impulses, to the spinal cord and brain, where neural arrangements lead to co-ordinated motor impulses back to the periphery. This is an important dimension of the sensorimotor image of the body, the image picturing activity in terms of sensation, central coordination and motion. There is a nervous circle. There is, to use cybernetic language, a constant feedback, a circle of living performance, analysable into sensory, central organizing and motor-executive functions.

The second broad body of research about motility starts, rather, with the centre, with the mind-brain initiating activity. Animals are active, and action is centrally initiated as well as a response to the external world; action is spontaneous and not only reactive. Reflecting this, ordinary speech refers to a human sense of action (in which someone 'makes a move'). It is a question, however, whether, how far and in what ways this sense is the outcome of central events, dependent on neural circuits in the brain, or the outcome of sensory impulses in nerves from the peripheral tissues to the brain resulting from moving actually carried out. It is probably a complex amalgam of both. And if there is a central sense of action, how is this to be understood? Inquiry raises complex psychological and philosophical issues about the nature of action and volition, or the will. At times, hard-nosed natural scientists have dismissed such issues and said that a science of an organism's movement, as a condition of being a *science*, eliminates reference to subjective feels of action or volition. Such scientists have pressed for exclusive adoption of the sensorimotor model. Yet, countering this position, are beliefs in the power of individual people to act voluntarily and even to exercise free will. These arguments greatly complicate any approach we may take to the sense of movement. To take them into account is, however, the right course, because agency and freedom to move clearly matter so much, so much of the time, to so many people. People *want* and *choose* to run, dance and move freely.

In order to describe and explain the sense of movement, it is necessary to consider the meanings of a number of terms. It is difficult to give clear-cut definitions, and the reasons why this is so turn out to be far from trivial. It is a fact that there is no consistency between different authors in use of the key terms relevant to awareness of self-movement – *kinaesthesia, proprioception, bodily sense* and *haptic sense*. It is also the case that a number of authors, recognizing that touch has many modalities, subsume the sense of movement under touch and then give it relatively little attention (e.g. Ratcliffe 2012). Yet, there are significant things to be said and distinctions to be made in connection with these terms. (The following historical chapter also considers these words, relating them to their origins.)

In the dictionary definition, kinaesthesia (or sometimes kinaesthesis) is 'the faculty of being aware of the position and movement of parts of the body, by means of sensory nerves (proprioceptors) within the muscles, joints, etc.: the sensation producing such awareness' (*OED* 2007, p. 1505). This definition encompasses both a narrow and precise and a broad and general usage. For the scientific psycho-physiologist, kinaesthesia is the conscious sensory accompaniment of the stimulation of receptors in muscles, joints, tendons and perhaps also skin that indicates a change in tension or extension in these tissues. The brain-mind (possessing, as the dictionary says, 'the faculty of being aware') organizes these stimuli into perceptions of the postural position or movement of the whole or of part of the body. At the same time, however, non-specialists use the word kinaesthesia loosely to cover the sense of movement and posture more generally. A host of other elements, apart from specific stimuli from muscles or joints, elements such as visual perceptions, volition, affect (or emotion), memory and learned habits, contribute to this sense. In such usage the word kinaesthesia bundles stimuli from the specific tissues effecting movement or affected by movement and posture together with other brain-mind activities. This makes kinaesthesia a descriptive term, with a scientific sounding ring, for general awareness of position and motility. Kinaesthesia, then, is 'the sensual perception of the position and movement of the body in relation to its surroundings' (Brandstetter et al. 2013, p. 7). Different writers refer, for instance, to 'kinesthetic practices' (Veder 2013, p. 5), 'bodily-kinesthetic intelligence', the body's ability to manage movement (Gardner 1993, pp. 206–237), 'kinesthetic empathy', a capacity to feel movement while observing the movement of others (Sklar 1994, p. 14; Foster 2011, pp. 6–11), to 'cultural modes of kinesthesia' (Brandstetter et al. 2013, p. 7), 'kinaesthetic imagination' (Reynolds 2007) and even to 'the kinesthetic citizen' (Steinman 2011). Ann Daly called dance 'fundamentally a kinesthetic art' (Daly 1992, p. 243). Susan Lanzoni's study of empathy was replete with references to 'kinesthetic imagery', 'kinesthetic modeling', 'kinesthetic sense' and so on (Lanzoni 2018). Both the narrow and the broad usages feature in contemporary discussion, and it is unhelpful to dismiss the broader usages as not understanding or deferring to science, since they draw attention to the fundamental role of awareness of movement in many valuable ways. I use the term kinaesthesia in the wider way, thereby placing the more precise or scientific usage in cultural context.

The word proprioception also needs comment. Sometimes it is used as a synonym of kinaesthesia. Gallagher, for instance, at one point referred to 'pre-reflective kinesthetic-proprioceptive experience' (Gallagher 2005,

p. 138). More often the words are differentiated, and proprioception then names the substantially non-conscious sensory nervous activity from different parts of the body with a place in posture and movement. The organs that originate the sensory stimuli are called proprioceptors. When proprioception becomes conscious, it might be called kinaesthesia. It is helpful to think of proprioception as primarily a physiological term (and I shall use it only in physiological context), and kinaesthesia as primarily a psychological one. But this distinction goes only so far, since the issue of differentiating physiological and psychological domains is itself so messy. Because there is a continuum of degrees of sensed movement from non-conscious proprioception, to 'pre-reflective self-consciousness' of movement (Gallagher and Zahavi 2021, p. 50), to full kinaesthetic self-consciousness, there is an inherent blurring of what is denoted by kinaesthesia and proprioception.

Proprioception, the non-conscious stimuli that report position and movement in the body, grading into conscious kinaesthetic awareness, shapes all sensory life, everything we sense. Sensing is embodied. The body is in the first instance not so much an object of perception for people (though it may be, especially when it does not work very well), but a constitutive principle of being a perceiving person. 'Proprioception is our totally intuitive sense of our own bodies without which we could not function at all, a kind of sixth sense which keeps our other senses in a balanced relation to each other' (Josipovici 1996, p. 110).

References to bodily feeling and bodily senses abound in everyday speech. These terms are valuable precisely because they are so general and ill-defined: they are family terms for the whole range of feelings that seem to belong to the body, like stomach ache, a full bladder, strain in the back, sensual pleasures, exercise and tiredness, warmth and coldness, and much more. The specialist literature sometimes refers to somesthesis or to coenaesthesia (a word more common in French) as more precise terms for bodily feelings. Specifying the source and causes of these feelings offers many challenges and requires the integration of studies of perception and emotion as well as physiology. Commonly enough, references to bodily feelings encompass touch and sensations connected with the body's, or body parts', posture and movements.

References to the haptic sense are, if anything, even more diverse than references to kinaesthesia and proprioception. In the humanities, for example, in art criticism, and in non-specialist writing about the perceptual world, the term characterizes belief that touch, with all its different modalities, including awareness of the body's state, posture and movements, contributes to perception generally, though most especially to visual perception. There is a great deal of contemporary discussion about the integration of the senses, including discussion of the importance of tactile qualities in what are customarily thought of as visual media, e.g. film or sculpture. Touch and movement, indeed, are in fact essential and continuously present elements in sight. Touch and movement notably inform the visual world of space and distance, as well as visual feel for the texture and solidity of things. Stressing the haptic character of vision therefore acknowledges that vision would really not be vision at all without the input of past and present touch. In turn, this understanding of vision contributes to the general conclusion, as a matter of fact, that there are not five clearly distinguishable senses – vision, hearing, taste, smell and touch – but that each sense helps constitute the others.

As with the other terms, there is no consistent usage of the word haptic. It is a generic term for the multifarious involvement of touch modalities in sensory life in general. For example, the influential psychologist of vision, J. J. Gibson, defined the haptic sense as 'the sensibility of the individual to the world adjacent to his body by the use of his body' and as 'the perceptual system by which animals and men are literally in touch with the environment' (Gibson 1966, p. 97). Having drawn attention to the crucial difference between active and passive touch in relation to learning about the world, he emphasized the role the body's activity has not just in touch but in vision (and the senses generally). Moving, a person (or animal) changes what there is to be perceived. Gibson went on to redescribe the world of objects perceived as a world of 'affordances': a person does not perceive neutral objects but actively perceives factors in the environment which have value or meaning and thus afford opportunities for living (Gibson 1979). We do not perceive a grey-brown rectangle with a matt or crumbly surface but a slice of bread affording the opportunity of eating.

Another reference to haptic sense which conferred authority on it in cultural and film studies originated with the philosopher Gilles Deleuze. The context was a discussion of different kinds of visual perception in life and in the arts involving both qualities of distance and the qualities of smoothness and striation. For such qualities, Deleuze (writing with Félix Guattari) claimed, '"haptic" is a better word than "tactile" since it does not establish an opposition between two sense organs [the eyes and tactile organs] but rather invites the assumption that that the eye itself may fulfill this nonoptical function' (Deleuze and Guattari 2004, p. 543). Adapting another usage spread by Deleuze, one might say that touch is 'folded' into sight.

Lastly, to round out this discussion of usage, it is necessary to note that the word haptics denotes the technological speciality of engineers and software designers building simulated touch mechanisms and working on digital 'feelies' (to parallel 'the movies'). 'Haptics', it has been said, 'declared the experimenter's power to capture, order, map, and represent the variety of sensations formerly grouped messily together under the heading of "touch"' (Parisi 2018, p. 143). Engineering touch sensibility, and especially the human-machine touch interface, has very large applications in robotics and prosthetics, though I shall not discuss this.

Different writers use key words differently. Gallagher and Dan Zahavi, for example, used kinaesthesia to denote the sense of movement and proprioception to denote the sense of posture and balance (Gallagher and Zahavi 2021). The writer on the senses, Mark Paterson, referred to 'kinaesthesis (the sense of movement), and proprioception (the sense of bodily position in space)', before going on to note that 'their status as distinct sense modalities is questionable' because of their integration in the organism's motility (Paterson 2021, p. 126). Some writers use proprioception to refer to everything in the domain of sensed movement. Barbara Montero, for instance, wrote on 'proprioception as an aesthetic sense' (Montero 2006). Robin Veder, in contrast, distinguished 'kin-aesthetic aesthetics' (Veder 2015). Robert Michael Brain, a writer on science and the modernist arts, treated the two terms as equivalent, referring to 'kinesthesia (eventually best known as proprioception): the sense of movement, balance; the sense of weight and resistance to the force of gravity, which give the body its sense of orientation in space' (Brain 2015, pp. 208–209). The philosopher Matthew Ratcliffe referred to kinaesthesia and proprioception together as making up 'body sense' (Ratcliffe 2012, p. 425). Thomas Fuchs, a psychiatrist, referred to 'the spatial body schema, proprioception, the sensations of movement or kinesthesia' (Fuchs 2021, p. 146).

All this emphatically shows that the words kinaesthesia, proprioception and haptic do not denote a single, localized bodily sense. Because of its complexity, there is no one right word to characterize the sense of movement. Much of the sense of movement comes, for example, from vision, and this is especially important in making a new movement. Gibson, for one, was clear about the complexity:

> There is articular kinesthesis for the body framework, vestibular [inner ear] kinesthesis for the movements of the skull, cutaneous kinesthesis for movement of the skin relative to what it touches,

and visual kinesthesis for perceptual transformations of the field of view. (Gibson 1966, p. 111)

Whatever the uses of the terms, the uses describe fundamental aspects of life. Gibson's work on perception led to the conclusion that what we might call environment-body is one living system (Gibson 1966). Moreover, the senses of touch and movement encompass the most primitive elements of the sensory world. They were very probably the first to appear in the evolutionary story and are thought to be the first to appear (well before birth) in individual development. It is surmised that the foetus feels the mother's breathing and heartbeat, and that when it kicks it feels the resistance of the enclosing womb. The earliest moving animals must have had some kind of proprioception in order successfully to move at all. As I shall explain, all this has a lot to do with the contribution of the sense of movement to the very notion of reality. The primeval character of the feel of movement surely also has much to do with the warmth of touching intimacy. What kind of emotional life would there be without touch, touch brought about in movement?

The sense of movement neither is nor could be the subject of only one research speciality but has a home in the psycho-physiological sciences of the senses in general and in the sciences of the control of posture and movement. Research, for instance, has provided description of sensory endings (the spindles) in muscles, in the tendons that tie muscles to bones, in joints and in skin (since folding seems also to be a source of knowledge of movement). It is difficult to know exactly how many types of sensory endings there are, where exactly they are located and which specialist function each has. The structures involved and the very fine nerves to which they are connected have proved hard to discern. There are also difficulties in investigating sensory modalities experimentally because the experimental subject's awareness of the body and the position of its parts is always present; this makes it difficult, or perhaps impossible, to isolate any one component of the sense of movement for rigorous study. In the brain, sensory input from muscles, joints or skin is integrated with information on balance from the middle ear and with information from the muscles of the eyeballs about the position and movement of the eyes. There is no centre for the sense of movement in the brain but a myriad of interconnections. Yet a unified awareness of movement is put together. We know the manner of standing and where 'we stand' in relation to our bodies and to our surroundings.

The sensory world, including kinaesthesia and proprioception, is essential to the motor side of the organism. The study of how people (and animals) control motility is a flourishing and complex research area. It is patent, for example, that conscious purposes encompass whole movements: a person greets someone with the gesture of a handshake or closes a door with a whole movement and not the separate contraction or relaxation of individual muscles. (We often enough do not have self-knowledge of which muscles are involved.) The brain possesses a model related to the future – an anticipation: given a purpose, the body, because of the model, 'knows' how it can be achieved. This, for instance, was the position of the influential Russian scientist of motor control, Nikolai Bernstein (Bernstein 1967). The presence of the model ensures that particular motor activity conforms to the wider living purposes of the animal or person.

Neural systems may explain the mechanisms involved in handshaking or door closing (to return to the previous examples) but they do not reveal why a particular person shakes the hand (or does not shake the hand) of another particular person at a particular time and in a particular place, or why a person closes the door (or maybe slams it). The world of human purposes, or intentions, requires other knowledge in order to be understood – knowledge of history, emotions, ethnicity, legality, aesthetics, education and so on. For this reason, it is as appropriate for a writer in the humanities to discuss movement and the feel of movement as for a natural scientist to do so. In fact, I say little further about the natural science of sensed movement. There is a place and a need for other forms of knowledge, not least in order to understand the social dimensions of kinaesthesia. Why dance indeed!

'The next step', however, is briefly to present relevant historical knowledge. Historical understanding is both knowledge in its own right and greatly helps appreciate the place felt movement has in modern life.

3 Kinaesthesia appears on the map

The history reveals the depth of the claims made for a close relation between touch and movement and *the feel for* reality.

Since ancient times, it has been the Western tradition to refer to *the five senses*: hearing, sight, taste, smell and touch. This makes it sound, unequivocally, as if there are five distinct senses, dependent on five separate sense organs in the ears, eyes, mouth, nose and skin. Yet, ordinary language also suggests a much less clear picture. It is common to refer to body senses (like temperature, or the feeling of a full stomach), the senses of pain and pleasure, the sense of balance, the sense of justice, common sense, a sense of reality, an intuitive sense, a sense of life, business sense, the moral sense and more. Moreover, from early on, commentators on the five senses recorded ways in which touch is different or special: the sense is not localized to a particular organ but distributed across the body surface and perhaps internally; it has many modalities or sensible qualities, like the feels of surface contact, texture, weight and pressure; and it appears to merge into a general feeling of being embodied or alive. It is no wonder that a twentieth-century assessment concluded that '"touch" serves as a blanket label for a very complex set of functions' (Jonas 1954, p. 510). There was also early discussion of whether touch should be considered necessary to the possibility of sensation in general and, therefore, the template of all the other senses. This came close to treating touch as the sense of life. Daniel Heller-Roazen, a professor of comparative literature, took over a Stoic phrase and presented this history as the history of 'the inner touch'. As he explored, scholars reasoned that there must be a 'common sense', a sense that unifies sensation, 'in which one perceives, in a single moment, a number of sensible qualities of different types' (Heller-Roazen 2007, p. 33). The common sense was thought to integrate the particular senses and thereby create a single picture of the object(s) of sense.

DOI: 10.4324/9781003368021-4

There are rich cultural histories and comparative anthropological studies of the senses and of the sensibility that the senses make possible. The senses are both capacities essential to animal existence and bearers of spiritual and moral lessons, and many studies amply confirm the large place of touch across time and around the world (Classen 2012). In all this study, however, there was until recently little about the sense of movement, and sometimes it was simply ignored.

Artists in a well-known European tradition painted allegories of the five senses in one picture or created sets of five paintings, one for each of the senses. In a set of paintings by Jan Breughel and Peter Paul Rubens early in the seventeenth century, the artists portrayed touch with a startling, even shocking, contrast.

Somewhat to right of centre from the viewer's vantage point a naked, voluptuous woman, with fine piled-up hair and wisps of covering, sits with bare feet on a carpet. She, Venus, turns, *moves*, to kiss the cupid she holds in her arms. Around her, and most especially at the left of the picture, are heaped up pieces of black metal armour, jagged, cold and unmoving, resting on a stone floor. Almost everyone will immediately see the socially conventional contrast between the tender, sensuous and feminine and the brutal, resistant and male forms of

Figure 3.1 Jan Breughel the Elder and Peter Paul Rubens. The sense of touch, 1618, detail. Oil on canvas. Museo del Prado, Madrid. In the public domain.

touch. But some viewers will be less observant of the fact that the woman is in motion; she turns (alive), while the armour sits there (dead). Were the armour to be in motion, it would be on a warrior actually employing physical power and symbolically wielding political power. The painting gives cause to remember that movement may be violent as well as intimate. As such painting proclaims, the language of the senses has done more than describe the physical body and its functions. Much follows from this. There can be no description of pure sensations as if they could exist in their own right as particular, separable things. Sensory and social worlds are interwoven.

Since Plato, it has been a rhetorical commonplace to refer to vision as 'the noble sense'. The senses have been bound up with social values, leaving a legacy with a lot of influence on how people have felt about bodily touch and movement. The judgment of the nobility of vision may have originated in the first instance from sight creating a feeling of distance between the observing soul and the objects which it observes. Distance, it was thought, makes it possible for the soul to take the lead in thinking or acting truly, unburdened by the closeness of passion. Sight, as opposed to the bodily activity of touching, or the enchantment or offence of smell, or powerful words or music, opens the possibility of acting calmly and rationally. The use of sight became associated with being objective, with not being confused or biased by subjective feelings of contact. The enormous number of measuring instruments with which scientists and engineers take 'readings' are a modern expression of this. The language of sight also fostered a highly gendered contrast between cold male reason and 'touchy-feely' female sensibility. A language of distance, of cool appraisal by sight, contrasts with the language of warm closeness, of reaction by feeling involving movement and touch.

There is a strong tendency nowadays to turn the ancient appraisal upside down and to view cool, distant relations, guided by objective standards, with suspicion or dislike and to rate highly contact by touch or, at least, by empathetic 'contact' through the feelings. A reference to 'cold reason' has negative connotations, 'warm contact' to positive ones. In sympathy with this, some writers on the senses in culture announce a supposed discovery, or recovery, of touch and movement as important to the arts and a lost, or at least seriously downplayed, dimension of human living. It is sometimes said that the West generally, or in other versions of the argument it is said that it is the modern age, has been oculocentric, obsessed with vision at the expense of the other senses (e.g. Levin 1993). Reference to the impact of photography, film and visual digital technologies bolsters this picture. From this point of view, it is then tempting to see signs that egalitarian ideals have replaced the nobility of sight with the humanity of touch. Yet, such large-scale generalities do not hold. There is ample evidence for the profound recognition of touch in all ages, as listing the figures of speech featuring movement has already indicated. The life of the senses is so rich and complex, and the senses so integrated, that to pick out one sense as culture-forming at the expense of the others seems artificial. Moreover, if in modern times people have re-established public touching, they have also elaborated rules fraught with emotion about not touching in the wrong place at the wrong time.

Sight has also been called noble because the eyes stand high on the person, lead the face, so to speak, look ahead, and, in romantic speech, open a window on the individual person or on the soul. The anatomical position of the eyes correlates with the evolution of upright posture, in all accounts a fundamental, if not the fundamental, step in humans becoming the dominant animal. Erwin W. Straus wrote a classic essay on this, drawing attention to the moral as well as material meaning of 'upright':

> Obviously, upright posture is not confined to the technical problem of locomotion. It contains a psychological element. It is pregnant with a meaning and not exhausted by the physiological tasks of meeting the forces of gravity and keeping the equilibrium. (Straus 1952, p. 530)

We 'look someone in the eye' in order firmly to engage with them; or we 'cast down' the eyes to avoid this or to show subservience or modesty. As this language confirms, description of the different senses has long been bound up with caste, class, gender and other forms of social differentiation. Sight requires 'the head', while 'the body' manages touch; reading and calculation is for the educated classes, work with the hands for others. References to the senses have reproduced the high-low, up-down, front-back hierarchy of the body, contrasting head and hand, reason and passion, refinement and brutality, civilization and primitiveness.

These general observations must serve to indicate the existence of a magnificently rich cultural background to the historical recognition of a specific sense of movement. The body senses and touch are at the centre of the story (Smith 2019a). The claims made for the new forms of natural philosophy in the seventeenth century, promulgated by the likes of Bacon, Galileo, Descartes and Newton, concentrated attention on the senses as well as on reason as sources of what could be known about the natural and human worlds. Emphasis on the senses as the source of knowledge, classically in John Locke's *An Essay Concerning Human Understanding* (1690), fostered closer inquiry into the character of the sense of touch and its relations to vision. There began to be more precise descriptions of the different sensory modalities; for instance, there were studies of sensing temperature and of balance (Wade 2003). Perhaps the single most important early contribution to discussion of touch was George (Bishop) Berkeley's *Theory of Vision* (1709). This acute and influential study brought touch into the analysis of vision, where it has remained ever since, arguing that touch is an essential component in the perception of three-dimensional space, space with distance. This was a model argument on the interconnectedness of the senses. Analyses of the different components of touch followed. At the same time, there was great medical and literary interest in the organization of bodily life and the sensibility and reactivity ('irritability') that marked this life. The developing genre of the novel gave this sensibility and reactivity a home in educated culture. The 'palpitations' (also a form of touch and movement) of Samuel Richardson's heroines, Pamela and Clarissa, fostered a European-wide audience avidly sharing an awareness of the power of the bodily senses.

Also in the eighteenth century, an increasingly precise philosophical literature linked touch with claims about the nature of physical reality. It was intuited, in touching and in the movement that brings touching about, that a person acting comes into contact with resistance, and that the feeling of action-resistance is the base or ground of knowledge of what is physically real. In movement and touch, it was claimed, an active 'I' encounters a resistant body or world. This, for instance, explains why the language of 'being in touch', of 'making contact' and of 'grasping reality' appears natural. Then, in the decades around 1800, a number of authors with medical and philosophical interests in the nature of life, like the English doctor-poet Erasmus Darwin, differentiated a sense specific to muscular movements. Writing in German, a number of such authors, including J. J. Engel and J. C. Steinbuch, discussed movements caused by the will, studied the role of movements in visual perception and referred to *Muskelsinn* (muscle sense). In the same years in France, the Revolution encouraged hopes for a 'science of Man' for the new age of the politically active citizen engaged in overcoming existing (resistant) conditions. Analysing the foundations for the science, intellectuals examined contact with reality in terms of sensibility for action-resistance, delineating action-resistance as the conceptual 'couple' (in Jean Starobinski's playful expression) fundamental to knowledge of the world through sensation (Starobinski 2003). One of the leaders of medicine in Paris, P.-J.-G. Cabanis, gave this systematic expression, linking mind and body in an integrated picture of sensible life. 'Touch', he declared, 'is the first sense to develop, the last which is extinguished. This is as it must be, since it is the base of the others, since it is, as it were, sensibility itself' (quoted in Smith 2019a, p. 77). He presumed that the first sense present in the embryo, touch, establishes awareness of action encountering resistance; this, he argued, is the basis for everything else that we know through sense about the world. Cabanis and his colleagues argued that the newly born human, moving and facing resistance to touch, differentiates a notion of self from a notion of world and on this base constructs knowledge. It was an enormously suggestive and influential way of thought. The philosopher and government servant, Maine de Biran, took this up and drew into the analysis the Christian image of a person possessing a voluntary will. A person, he argued, has a direct, irrefutable intuition of free active power. This is volition. This active power, he explained, comes up against the resisting body and world, and this is the source of feeling and knowledge. Over a century later, this foundational image of human freedom enacted and resisted entered into the existentialist vision of the human condition.

There was also recognition in these years of the existence of a sense of movement caused by contracting muscles and moving limbs. At least one writer, the London teacher of anatomy and anatomical artist, Charles Bell (later, Sir Charles), ennobled this sense as 'a sixth sense'. Publishing in 1816, he wrote: 'Was I willing to break in upon the received opinions in an elementary book [a textbook for medical students], I would say that there was a sixth sense, the most important of all, the sense of motion' (*The Anatomy and Physiology of the Human Body*, quoted in Smith 2019a, p. 105). He called this sixth sense 'the muscular sense'. (I quote at length as the standard *OED* cites a later source.)

> It is [the touch] sense which gives correctness to all the others, at least if we are right in attributing so much to the exercise of this sense; as hardness, softness, solidity, figure, extension and motion. If the sense of touch be that change arising in the mind from the application of external bodies to the skin, then certainly the organ has high exercise, and is of all the senses the most valuable. But it appears to me that these qualities ... belong to what I would call the muscular sense, that conception of distance which we acquire

by moving our body or our members, by pressing upon an object and feeling the resistance it occasions. Much might be said on the subject. (quoted in Smith 2019a, pp. 113–114)

Indeed, much was to be said on the subject. Reference to the sixth sense, in the manner in which Bell adopted this expression, can indeed still be found: 'Proprioception is the ... "sixth sense" that allows me to know whether my legs are crossed or not, without looking at them' (Gallagher and Zahavi 2021, p. 162). Alain Berthoz entitled a chapter, 'The sense of movement: a sixth sense?' (Berthoz 2000, chapter 2). John Martin, writing on performance and dance, referred to a human 'sixth sense', kinaesthesia (Martin 1936, p. 110); Josipovici described 'a kind of sixth sense ... More basic than sex or even desire, proprioception is the body's sense of itself as occupying space and as active in that space' (Josipovici 1996, p. 110). Modern references to 'the sixth sense', though, may be to very different things. While they may refer to kinaesthesia, they more commonly denote a 'sense' connecting obscure bodily feelings and intuition, or they denote a capacity for extrasensory perception (ESP). Googling the phrase leads to a site about a 1999 film in which a boy communicates with the dead.

Between about 1800 and 1830, discussion of the existence and nature of a specific sense of movement, which a number of authors called the muscular sense, took off. The muscular sense was put on the map for people interested in physiology and psychology, and it became a research topic in science in its own right. Bell's investigations were to prove notably significant, as he tied his claims about the existence of a muscular sense to a postulated 'circle of nerves' connecting muscles to the brain, a circle in which a muscle receives a motor stimulus from the brain to contract and the brain receives a sensory stimulus from the muscle in return, conveying information about the muscle's state of contraction and hence information about an action or movement. This located the sense of movement, understood as a sense of the contracted or relaxed condition of muscle, in the functional context where it has remained in science, central to the body's regulation and control of posture and locomotion. Working out of the details of the mechanisms involved became an ongoing project of enormous complexity.

During the nineteenth century, the study of all the senses became topics of specialized psycho-physiological research, for the most part with each sense treated independently. The research encompassed both perception of other things moving – research influential in the development of motion pictures late in the century – and perception of self-movement. Investigations of the sense of self-movement relied heavily on clinical data, on cases of loss or damage to nervous functions, though there were also experimental studies. Bell and others reported the model case of a young woman who was able to hold her child in a normal way, but only so long as she looked at it; if she looked away, she dropped the child. This was persuasive evidence for the existence of a muscular sense; if it is absent, there is a dramatic effect on a person's capacity to maintain normal posture and movement. It became common knowledge that there is a distinctive sensory world in the muscles and limbs, even if much of this world is generally non-conscious.

Reference in medicine and sciences of the mind to the existence of the muscular sense was standard in English by about 1830. It was by no means settled, however, what exactly it was a sense of, nor what bodily and mental processes were actually involved. Some researchers thought that the muscular sense was, as Bell had described it, the result of a specific sense organ in muscles sending sensory impulses through the nerves to the brain. Others, like the Berlin physiologist Johannes Müller, thought it closely connected with the awareness people said they had of effort, an awareness of being the initiator of movement, and they deduced that the muscular sense, at least in part, accompanied motor impulses from the brain to muscles. Another German physiologist, E. H. Weber, influentially connected muscular feeling to the question of the perception of weight, and he elaborated methods to bring experimental studies to bear on the issues. But there was no closure of discussion, no agreed synthetic theory. Potentially different topics were treated together, and there was a confused mixture of reference to factors like the will, appropriate to discussion of mind, and to factors like the coordination of muscles, appropriate to discussion of body.

Seeking to bring to an end interminable argument about clinical and experimental evidence concerning the muscular sense, in 1880 the London neurologist, H. Charlton Bastian, introduced the term 'kinæsthesis', which he defined simply as 'sense of movement' (Bastian 1880, p. 543). Bastian was convinced that Bell had been essentially correct: there is a specific sense of movement arising from limb motility and posture, a sense sending sensory information to the brain. Drawing on Greek roots, he called this sense kin-aesthesis, or the motion sense. Publishing in a book for a non-specialist audience, his word in English quickly caught on, though the uptake was much slower in other languages. In Russian, for example, the physiologist Ivan Sechenov introduced muscular sensation under the broader heading of 'dark sense' or 'dark feeling', affirming the connections of sensed movement with the bodily senses in general. Through the last half-century of tsarist rule and throughout the Soviet years, this was the language in terms of which Russian physiologists knew about kinaesthesia (Smith 2019b). In the last decade of the nineteenth century, Bastian's view of the peripheral sensory source of kinaesthesia won the scientific debate at the expense of theories attributing a sense of action or movement to central brain impulses, though this success was more clear-cut in the English-speaking than in the French-speaking world (Clarac et al. 2009). From then on, there was continuous research on the special nerve endings in muscles and on nerve endings in tendons and joints, and on their place in the coordination of muscular action, posture and locomotion (Mayer 2020).

Around 1900, the intensely professional standards expected in physiology and the emergence of psychology as an academic and scientific discipline together encouraged the separation of *physiological* questions about nervous organization and muscular control from *psychological* questions about will, perception, action and attention. (The theory of the neuronal basis of the nervous system was shaped in the 1890s.) In this context, the psychologists appropriated the word kinaesthesia. In the first two decades of the twentieth century, especially in the United States, they showed considerable interest in understanding the contribution of sensed movement to cognition in general as well as to motility in particular. The physiologists, in contrast, concentrated on investigating neural processes while keeping at a distance claims about mental functions. They left psychological issues, like the place in the conscious sense of movement (or kinaesthesia) of stimuli that are customarily non-conscious, for the future. Both psychology and physiology became specialized sciences, and issues like the nature of the muscular sense lost almost any connection with public culture in which people valued and thought about self-movement. Nevertheless, it was common knowledge that there is a special sense related to posture, balance and movement. The earlier cluster of assumptions linking touch, movement and the sense of reality also retained a public hold.

The English physiologist C. S. Sherrington contributed the term proprioception to this demarcation between psychology and physiology. His lectures at Yale University, published in 1906 as *The Integrative Action of the Nervous System*, was a major synthesis of experimental work and theoretical thinking about how the nervous system serves the unity of the organism. The book was to be cited for half a century in the English-speaking world for laying out a programme of research linking rigorous study of events at the level of the neurons in the spinal cord with a theoretical ideal in which the nervous system was understood to function as a whole. Sherrington supported the promotion of psychology as a science but, writing as a physiologist, he discussed psychology only in circumscribed ways. Indeed, seeking for physiologically appropriate terms with which to discuss the bodily sensory world ('interior' sensation), as opposed to the world of the five senses ('exterior' sensation), he drew on Latin roots and coined the term 'proprio-ception' (Sherrington 1961, p. 132). His word denoted the system of nervous stimuli originating in the body, considered from a physiological point of view. He discussed phenomena which earlier researchers had called muscular sense in terms of the largely non-conscious sensory elements of the body's nervous system for controlling posture and movement. Nevertheless, in spite of this historical root, and in spite of the very largely non-conscious nature of proprioceptive activity, some writers (e.g. Maurette 2018) persist in referring to proprioception as a 'sense'. This once again illustrates the capacity of thought about the sense of movement to disrupt language that might keep mind and body in separate discourses.

Scientists early in the twentieth century began to appreciate that reflex-action models of nervous organization were not adequate to account for the complexity and, above all, adaptive flexibility of the living, moving organism. Sherrington, however much his experimental programme of research concerned the nervous pathways of specific reflexes, elaborated the concept of integration in order to relate his own and similar work to the subtlety evident in living activity. In Russia, in the 1920s and 1930s, Bernstein improved techniques (pioneered by Muybridge and Marey in the nineteenth century) for the film recording and analysis of movements (chronophotography). Impressed by the flexibility of the body in achieving the movements a person sets out to achieve, he opposed Pavlov's theory of reflexes and proposed instead that, for effective action, there must be a central model or schema. When institutional power in Pavlov's name in the Soviet empire declined in the 1960s, and when Bernstein's work was translated, this work became one of the foundations of current research on movement control.

Research has become ever more specialized, though in basic shape it has built on earlier approaches. There has been more and more appreciation of the complexity and refinement of the mechanisms involved in touch and movement. There may, for example, be at least thirteen different types of sub-surface nerve endings active in contact touch. Perhaps the most significant new development, however, was not a discovery but a result of the crossing of disciplinary boundaries.

An institutional and intellectual change, plainly visible from around 1980, has made it commonplace to argue, as concerns knowledge of mind (however mind is understood), that psychology, physiology and philosophy need each other. The outcome, deeply bound up with the new technology and political economy of computing, has been the massive growth and influence of the neurosciences. As a result, contemporary thought about the sense of movement owes much to a number of scientific and philosophical specialities. This makes an overview a challenge.

An exclusively biological view portrays proprioception as a function necessary for the realization of movement and posture. This leaves it unclear what to say about kinaesthesia, or the conscious sense of movement: 'the importance of conscious proprioception for movement remains unclear' (Tuthill and Azim 2018, unpaginated). Why, biologically, should there be conscious as well as non-conscious regulation of movements? The question gives particular form to the old difficulty of dualist views of body and mind, the difficulty of saying what consciousness is for.

One constructive development is a shift in the direction of research from the study of individual organs of sense to their integration. For many decades, the highly technical nature of research on visual and auditory senses encouraged specialized work on each sense, or on a modality of each sense (e.g. on perception of colour separately from form). Nevertheless, scientists had long recognized the limits of such narrowing of focus, aware, to take a significant example of sensory interaction, of the central contribution of eye movements to visual perception of space and distance. Gibson's research on active touch perception drew him into representing the sensory system as an integrated whole. Analytic philosophical studies, as well as psychological research, showed just how difficult it is to define a sense or to say exactly how many senses there are. Indeed, 'it is a notoriously difficult project to individuate the senses' (Fulkerson 2014, p. 13). This has spread the view that conventional references to 'the five senses' are just that – conventional. It is a view very receptive to enlarged discussion of the sense of movement.

A number of interests have contributed to radical critique of distinctions between the senses and to the literature on haptic sensation sensitive to this. This is especially evident in art and installations that explore multimedia performance, and also in haptics, engineering tactile sensation with roots in technologies like Braille, enabling the blind 'to see' through moving the touching fingers. The art world has shown considerable interest in multisensory processes in performances which combine video, dance and sound. There is also experimentation on synaesthesia, sensory experience in which one sense normally thought to be the source of particular modes of sensation gives rise to sensations associated with another, for example, when there is hearing through vibrations felt by the feet or seeing through the finger tips. While multisensory processes are the norm in psychological life, synaesthesia is very individual and sometimes truly exceptional in character.

The following movement brings psychological and philosophical questions into sharper focus.

Part II

Second movement: andante

4   A feel for reality

This chapter examines the intuition that moving, acting against resistance, gives a person a feeling for what is real. Asking whether something really exists, you may be most persuaded that it does if you can touch it. It is a way of judging reality which comes with the highest authority. When Thomas saw Christ appear after the resurrection, he doubted what he saw. 'Doubting Thomas' made the surely unsurprising demand: 'Except I shall see in his hands the print of the nails, and put my finger into the print of the nails, and thrust my hand into his side, I will not believe' (Bible, John, 25). Christ offered his resurrected body to human touch (which required movement, 'to put', 'to thrust') in order to confirm its reality. In the mid-eighteenth century, Dr Johnson famously claimed to refute Berkeley's philosophical idealism by saying, 'I refute it thus' while strenuously *striking* a large stone with his foot (as reported by Boswell, quoted in Smith 2019a, p. 63). Who doubts the physicality of the stone resisting movement? These kinds of statements give philosophers pause, however, since in logic it would seem that the sense of contact is no more a guarantee of something being real than any other sense. As a number of critics (like the Oxford philosopher F. H. Bradley) have pointed out, much might be said for pain sensations, rather than sensed movement, as direct revelations of something appropriately called real. What could be more real than pain (or, indeed, intense pleasure)? So, we should be wary of concluding that action-resistance is the origin of knowledge of the real, as opposed to a source of culturally bound feel for what is real. This said, it has been the norm in English to attribute confidence in feeling about reality to the consequences of touch. Since, as I stress, touch involves movement and the sensibility that goes with it, there is reason, to a significant degree, to trace this feel for physical reality to kinaesthetic sense. Historically, numerous authors have discerned the 'I' inescapably

DOI: 10.4324/9781003368021-6

bound-up in a world by its action and by resistance to it, by movement and opposition to movement.

Johnson, in kicking a stone and in other ways, memorably gave a voice to common sense. This reference to common sense is to a widely shared belief, so taken for granted by people in a particular community that its rejection appears silly or mad. The claim, then, is that touch, along with the sensibility to movement that brings touch about, has had a large place in common-sense (Western and modern) notions of reality. It has also been the subject of much considered philosophical reflection. Writing after Johnson, Cabanis' French colleague, Destutt de Tracy, seeking the basis in knowledge for social theory, wrote: 'the property of resistance to our will to move is thus at the base of all that we learn to know' (quoted in Smith 2019a, p. 76). Maine de Biran, a close reader of his work, then emphasized that the actual exercise of activity, an act of will, comes first and precedes the feeling of resistance, and that the two together then make possible the notion that there is an ego, the 'I' or self:

> Each movement, each step made is a very distinct modification which affects me doubly – by itself and by the act which determines it... These indeed are the two terms of the relation which are necessary for the foundation of this first simple judgment of personality, *I am*. (Maine de Biran 1929, p. 55)

These were the roots of an influential strand in French philosophy. In the words of the twentieth-century historian and philosopher of science, Georges Canguilhem, 'consciousness requires the conflict of a power and a resistance' (Canguilhem 1994, p. 374). To use a word with very considerable ramifications, at the base of conscious life, it has been maintained, is a *dialectic*, action and resistance to action, power and opposing power, in which the polarity is the condition of possibility for reflective consciousness and language.

The quotation from Maine de Biran attributed the origin of the subjective notion of the self to dialectically related elements, an active power and resistance to it; that is, he stated that belief in the reality of the ego is the result of deductive inference from the elementary awareness given in the action-resistance couple. Yet he, as also some later philosophers, also wrote as if the notion of the self is present in the very constitution of active consciousness, that is, as if the self is given, inherent in a human being the kind of subject a human being is. This ambivalence continues to be debated in phenomenological writings. The ambivalence, however, is not important in ordinary speech or in writing on developmental psychology which relates the feeling for the reality of the self to the subjective world of felt activity-resistance. We may, for present purposes, put to one side further analysis of the self concept.

Ask yourself, why do you feel real? The answer will very likely include reference to the fact that you have, and you know you have, a body, or, speaking more precisely, that you are *embodied*. You know this because you feel your body and you move, and the body both executes the movement and resists it. Ill people in particular know a lot about resisting bodies. And when people claim that they do not feel real, we may wonder what kind of illness or disturbance, or perhaps virtual reality technology, is making them unaware of their own bodies.

Concern with the source of knowledge in felt action-resistance was of course not a French monopoly. It is also strongly illustrated, for example, in the writing of the Berlin philosopher, Wilhelm Dilthey, author of canonical studies of knowledge in the humanities. Dilthey was at the heart of debate on the differences between explaining physical nature and explaining human nature and culture. In 1890, he argued: 'Only for a consciousness aware of volitional impulses and resistance can something actual be given, can there be matter and finally our earth within a universe of celestial bodies'. And, further, 'impulse and resistance are seminal for the separation of self and object' (Dilthey 2010, pp. 35, 44). As explained by Rudolf Makkreel, a translator and editor of his work, this argument led to belief that 'the bodily felt resistance to our will that derives from the world around us also incorporates our relation to other human beings' (Makkreel 2022, p. 126):

> The emotional and volitional processes that here give color and strength to the reality of other life-units consist of dominance, dependence, and community. Through them we gain the lived experience of a *thou*, which at the same time deepens the sense of the *I*. A constant slight change of pressure, resistance, and support causes us to feel that we are never alone. (Dilthey 2010, p. 29)

Human action and resistance to action puts a person into relation with things, events and other people. Actions and resistances form the social, political and moral worlds people inhabit, as well as the physical ones. Following up his discussion of Dilthey, Makkreel therefore drew attention to the connection between Dilthey's statement and the language of the Christian existentialist, Martin Buber.

Buber discussed the moral quality of human relationships in terms of whether a person experiences an other as a 'thou' rather than a 'you', or, put another way, as a personal subject rather than an impersonal object. The evaluative content of action-resistance, as Dilthey interpreted its phenomenology, is ethically real, forming (in Buber's language) the distinction in relations between a 'thou' and a 'you', a distinction basic to moral feeling.

Discussion of the feel for reality gives insight into why movement like dance matters. The establishment of something, some event or someone as real is central to the significance that things and people possess. Moving and coming up against bodies, things and people forms the world as it matters to an individual person or groups of people. Dance movement gives this aesthetic form.

The same conclusion can be reached from a very different starting point in psychoanalytic thought. Before birth, the child and the mother are in large respects one integrated organism. The foetus, however, begins to make some movements of its own after about eight weeks, and it is probable that it then develops some kind of sensory awareness, perhaps through movement and resistance, or through pressure or from the rhythm of the mother's heartbeat and breathing. Such sentience is unarguably present at and immediately after birth. It was the large contribution of Melanie Klein to focus on the early days and to attribute to them the formative experiences shaping the character of the child and adult. The essential process – I simplify – is said to be that the initial pleasurable or painful, satisfying or frustrating, quality of the baby's contact with the mother, and subsequently with other caregivers, establishes an appreciation of the nature of a relationship. The earliest experiences form a model against which the individual tests and judges all subsequent forms of 'contact'. The child projects the image it has of its first relationship onto the world of other things and people. (Thus, the stock joke that a boy seeking close relations with a girl seeks his mother.) Children deprived of actual contact, as painful stories from orphanages and dire backgrounds attest, may develop an incapacity for good qualities in relationships. Therapists tackle the difficulties people have relating to each other and to themselves, and the pain that certain kinds of relations cause, by reconstructing the roots of relations in the early days of movement and resistance.

If one accepts some form of this persuasive argument, then one may think of movement as the template for the formation of relations of all kinds. Donald Winnicott's theory of transitional objects, for instance, understood the attachment of young children to an object, such as a blanket or a soft toy, as the projection onto an object of affective qualities earlier found in attachment to the mother. The object effects the achievement of a child's wider relations. Such views then make it possible to connect the theory of transition to the empirical study of touch practices, implicating kinaesthesia and the acquisition of a geography of things in the formation of a person (Volvey 2012). Winnicott and other analysts also associated the earliest movements of the foetus with movements later interpreted as aggression, thus associating the sense of movement with core emotional/affective experience. For Winnicott, the very activity that shows that an embryo is alive sets up the pattern of aggression fundamental to personality: 'A baby kicks in the womb... A baby of a few weeks thrashes away with his arms ... A baby chews the nipple with his gums; it cannot be assumed that he is meaning to destroy or to hurt. At origin aggressiveness is almost synonymous with activity' (Winnicott 1958, p. 204). Moving, the baby produces a response, and the sense of this, perfused with emotion, is the core of the subjective world.

If the early days before and after birth lay down patterns of relations which shape all of a person's subsequent life, then the pattern of experienced movement enters every aspect of a person's character and social relations.

As people move, so they are. For Maxine Sheets-Johnstone, a philosopher and a former dancer, who argued at length about the centrality of sensed movement, 'we humans learn "which thing we are" by moving and listening to our own movement' (Sheets-Johnstone 2011, p. 49).

We might wonder about the difference new reproductive technologies will make. If babies are born from one woman's body and then cared for by another, or if babies come to birth in an artificial and extremely expensive womb ('in a test-tube', as humour has it), will their felt movements and resistances, and hence the quality of their relations, differ? Some readers will recall fearfully how Frankenstein gave birth to his monster. The monster was not 'born of a woman' (Bible, Job, 14) but assembled, like a machine in a factory, from parts torn from cadavers, brought together and then made alive by electricity. We might also speculate about the effects of tightly swaddling young infants, as Russian peasants, for example, used to do. It protected babies from people or animals, the cold and the dangers of the stove in one-room peasant houses, yet we may feel it deprived children of the movement they want and need.

This leads to questions about the effects on the sense of movement, and with it, the sense of reality, of new digital technologies, which had

Figure 4.1 Danya and Natasha. Photograph, in the author's collection. By kind permission.

increased importance almost overnight with the onset of the COVID-19 pandemic. Social media, that is social 'contact' using IT rather than by coming together in a common physical space, as well play with virtual realities, have become commonplace. Enforced isolation during the pandemic speeded up the changes, not least by transferring online everyday 'contact' in teaching and business. What, then, do we know about the differences in self-presentation (including gesture and posture) and feelings of identity, movement and reality when people share physical space and when they relate 'at a distance' via electronic media? Though it may still be early objectively to assess the changes, there is a wealth of impressionistic evidence about how changes in the sense of movement change the feel for reality.

The changes may be positive: a person watching TV sees actors in a theatre or footballers in a stadium in far more detail than if the person were physically present in the theatre or stadium (except for the few with expensive tickets). Further, the performance can be repeated at will. On Zoom, people from around the world participate without having to buy flights, obtain visas and wasting days in airports. Working at home avoids commuting. No one touches inappropriately online. New and un-anticipated aesthetics excite and challenge artists. Visual media permit, and may enhance, appreciation of another person's movement. So, why doesn't everyone just settle down at home and enjoy the new media?

With this question, discussion of the feel for reality kicks in. Everyone was once a baby and everyone has a body, and that past and this present is there, and people are aware that it is there through movement, contact and resistance in memory and in actuality. It is commonplace to recognize 'bodily memory', the kind of memory in which the body unconsciously 'knows' what to do in a habitual action (Koch et al. 2012). Videos display movement, sometimes beautiful movement, but this movement is at one 'remove' from the way each person originally felt movement. A small experiment may help appreciate this. Watch yourself move in a mirror; then take away the mirror and look 'inside yourself' as you move. Removing the mirror is precisely what certain studios of early modern dance encouraged, self-consciously rejecting ballet training. There is a different perception of movement seen as it would be seen 'in the eyes of others' and subjectively seen 'in oneself'. Felt movement is real in both cases, but the modern dancers who removed the mirror claimed that they gained access to a more natural, deeper or truer personal reality than the ballet dancer who was not concerned with the feel of movement for the self but with the look of movement for another. While we may think that the contrast is not so straightforward, it is the case that the different contexts of movement, including the shift to online 'contact', affect the feel for reality. Without question, feelings, claims and customs about what is said to be real change. It is therefore striking to find many instances of people, even young people highly familiar with electronic forms of 'contact', choosing to have physical presence when possible. Students opted after the pandemic to return to lectures in their institutions, to meet in cafes, to hang out, to embrace; dance companies reassembled in common physical spaces with conspicuous relief and joy. Josipovici told an insightful anecdote. A friend had returned from visiting Rome: 'But why, I asked him, had he not been content merely to see, why had he felt the need to *touch*? "I don't really know", he said, and then: "I suppose touching something confirms its presence"' (Josipovici 1996, p. 59).

An intellectually smart young computer programmer comes to visit. He works all day at his job, which involves programming a kind of virtual reality so that pilots can learn safely how to handle aircraft. At the end of the day, he affirms, professional programmers have a strong desire to have contact with 'the real world' (his phrase), to return to real as opposed to virtual presence, to have contact in physical space with things and people. What is not real about the visual and aural electronic realities so that he cannot take them seriously as reality? It is not easy to answer this question, especially when it concerns electronic communication between people in which images of interlocutors move, gesture, talk, perform and give pleasure and pain, just like physically present people.

Generalities, it is necessary to accept, break down. If for many people there is greater formality in online relations and less spontaneity or play, for others there is liberation. But it is still possible to map effects as they concern movement.

To start with, the digital image is not an image of the whole person; there is often not even a picture of the whole body, and there is no third dimension, so important to appreciation of depth, weight and solidity and hence appreciation of a person's physicality. The image is usually not the size of a person. There is certainly no smell. Then, online, there is no possibility to touch. To be sure, when people are physically present to each other there may also be no touching; indeed, it may be strictly controlled. Its absence, online or offline, may bring on feelings of deprivation, which vary in vividness and power in either circumstance. All the same, a tactile imagination colours the relations a person has with things and people online and offline, though this imagination is often more vivid or pressing when there is physical presence. A person sees another person move online or offline, and the other person sees the movement of the first. But dialogue in movement feels rather 'detached' offline. There is opportunity on video to see wonderful movers, which might be very difficult to see live, yet online movers are 'at a distance', which is an emotional 'distance' as well as a physical one. It is not just a matter of physical space but of imaginative space, and there seems to be a gradation in imagination for closeness, linked to physical presence or absence. Moreover, the online image comes framed, which is a marked signal that it is in some sense artificial. Online, a considerable part of the geography, or setting, of a person's life is absent, and the penumbra of sensations jostling at the edges of awareness in presence is definitely diminished. There are differences in the mode of listening and of gaze. Then there is the question of sound. Online sound is often not that good and is a central reason why online users frequently devote much time and concentration to handling the technology rather than to communicating with each other. Silences abound. When two or more people come together, the repertoire of movement and gesture of the whole body participates. There may be considerable unanticipated activity. Online, people report, there is less gesture, less spontaneity; others, though, report opportunities for surprise and novelty, with less embarrassment or modesty. When teachers teach or lecture online, they do not see the audience; they are very uncomfortable speaking into 'empty space'. Good speaking has the audience in mind: it invites a response, and the speaker seeks that response, even if in the form of a silent but visible audience. The gesture of speech seeks out the gesture of receptivity, and this is badly disturbed online. Summing up, Fuchs referred to an atmospheric feeling of presence which is lost online (Fuchs 2021, p. 99).

Experimentation with virtual reality exists alongside IT. Having fun with or artistically exploring virtual reality depends on the contrast virtual reality offers with 'real' reality. However sophisticated the machine which mediates reality, the body of the subject interacting with the machine remains present. If you try to imagine a machine replacing all the senses at once, what kind of presently imaginable machine would replace bodily and proprioceptive sentience, that is, would replace the body with all its biochemistry, hormones, breathing, posture and movement? Our programmer says that professionals like himself who work with virtual reality are especially sensitive to the difference between virtual and 'real' reality and want to return to the latter after work. Following up Fuchs's argument leads to the conclusion that it is above all the presence and absence of resistance, experienced in kinaesthetic sensibility, which makes the difference between actual and virtual realities.

It is in fact the almost perfect visual, tactile, and motoric coupling between user and computer that circumvents the experiences of resistance and foreignness that are characteristic of our normal bodily encounters with the world. This manifests itself not least in concepts such as 'internet surfing,' 'browsing,' or 'skimming': they indicate the *minimization of resistance* in a medium that offers limitless possibilities for movement and, thus, an almost omnipotent self-experience. (Fuchs 2021, p. 96)

If kinaesthetic perception changes in using virtual reality technologies, proprioception persists, and hence a person is able to tell the difference between actual and virtual realties. Of all the senses, it is sight that most enables escape from the resistances of the world (hence in part the deep appeal of film); it is kinaesthesia and proprioception that return a person to face the couple, action-resistance.

All these points have a place in understanding why there is a continuing, or renewed, desire for live performance in the sports and in the arts. Why should this be, in addition to the interest theatres, companies, teams and stadiums have in getting a financial return on investment and in providing many people with a living? Audiences certainly desire to participate in social events or rituals, but is it only a matter of habit and custom which makes people want to be with other people in a physical sense? If it is, give social change time, and let an older generation that has difficulty adapting die out, and 'contact' via digital media will not just be sufficient for, but will embellish, human relations.

Well, no. The post-COVID reaction showed that people feel embodiment and want physical presence. Kinaesthesia enters into this. The objection to life online boils down to the existential claim that humans are embodied and that bodies are mobile in three dimensions, or four if you think of time as a dimension. The full encounter with a person involves a moving body, not only an image of a body. A body and an image of a body have a different history as well as a different kind of presence; they come bearing different legacies, and these matter. Moreover, a body and an image of a body have a different future: the former dies, and a live performance flares up and is gone, while images may be recorded and preserved.

Also consider haptics. In due course, we may suppose, manufacturers will market everyday products communicating touch. This will probably produce a lot of sensual entertainment and make a lot of money. It does not seem likely, however, that new devices, anymore than those in existing use, will persuade people that a tactile image of a person is the real person. There is more to the feeling of touch than the sense of literal contact with surfaces, and this 'more' exists because touch encompasses the body senses, including the sense of movement. The new devices will have to be very good indeed to reproduce the complexity and range of the body senses and proprioception.

> Compared to ordinary visual and auditory sensations, haptics is difficult to synthesize. Visual and auditory sensations are gathered by specialized organs, the eyes and ears. On the other hand, a sensation of force can occur at any part of the human body, and is therefore inseparable from actual physical contact. These characteristics lead to many difficulties in developing a haptic interface. (Hiroo Iwata, quoted in Parisi 2018, p. 262)

When the social context is appropriate, it is common for people to want to come together. They do: for funerals as well as weddings, to go to boxing matches as well as to go to bed. Lockdown, quarantine and isolation during the pandemic almost at once gave rise to reports about the psychological costs to individuals: loneliness, depression, domestic violence. Going online was not enough. 'Getting together' (a lot of movement is implied in this phrase) simply is part of well-being. Certainly, there is a spectrum of means enabling people to be with each other, ranging from media which communicate at a distance, when it is possible only to hear or see, to forms of physical presence in which there is a feeling of proximity, to actual contact, which itself varies on a scale from the formal handshake to the intimate kiss. When any kind of media *mediates*, there is something different than the wholeness of a close person. Even person to person talk is not a caress.

A face-to-face encounter or a live performance is *an event*: it happens and, whatever follows, it, with its particularity, is then over. Of course, recording is common. But there is a quality, even a frisson, in the live encounter or performance that cannot be repeated. The live encounter or performance, like life itself, passes. The temporality of physical presence, like embodiment, is an existential condition, not something that can be changed without changing what it is to be human.

I continue throughout to argue a point repeatedly made: contact is 'con-tact', a coming together, a movement both at one and the same time physiological, psychological, moral and social. The next chapter describes this more closely. It involves characterizing in a more systematic way the feel of movement and the intuitive feel for reality with which it is so closely associated. For this, the resources of phenomenology are needed.

5 Phenomenology and embodiment

When you feel you move, well, you feel movement. Movement is 'there'. Everyday descriptions of this 'thereness' of movement are extremely rich. A person might refer to a feeling of change taking place in spatial relations (poking a head through a window); or to a feel something is changing in time as well as space (like stretching a leg); or to a sense of reality ('striking' confirms the stone is real, or moving an arm means it is not broken). The movement may be said to belong to a body (e.g. a 'movement of the bowels'), or a person may claim to originate the movement and say, 'I move'. The movement may feel like a free action, or it may fail because of resistance. It may seem like 'a wise move' or it may seem unfortunate ('I was led a fine dance'). Descriptions of the subjective feel of movement assign character to the 'thereness' of the movement, and they report that this has significance in some particular way for a person. The analysis of such descriptions belongs to phenomenology.

Phenomenology is not equivalent to introspection, which reports the feel of a state within a particular person, as it seeks proper description of the general form or structure of conscious life rather than description of a particular person's subjective world. The phenomenological project in philosophy is to go beyond description to explanation of subjective, intuitive experience in terms of the rationally or logically necessary structure and character of the conscious world of being. The present task, however, is more limited.

Proprioception, sensory information from the body, is always present as part of the background of mental life. As such, reference to it necessarily has a place in phenomenological description, description which encompasses the embodied nature of the mental world. This embodied nature is not simply a neutral matter of fact (if there were such a thing) but establishes meaning in the conscious world. Ordinary speech describes the intuition of posture or movement as belonging to

DOI: 10.4324/9781003368021-7

an 'I', and movement has meaning for a person who moves. Indeed, Berthoz and Jean-Luc Petit (the former a physiologist of the brain, the latter a phenomenologist) made the very strong claim that awareness of being an embodied 'I' essentially depends on the presence of bodily movement: 'the attribution of a meaning of being to our own body depends essentially upon kinaesthesia' (Berthoz and Petit 2008, p. 227). This is a claim that makes kinaesthesia not just a central component but essential in any kind of talk about the human person. Sitting, walking or dancing, a person feels the place and movement, say, of the hip, and that phenomenon goes into forming the world as the world exists for the person; it is there as part of a particular life. Phenomenological description seeks objective terms in which to characterize this subjective world.

Consider a moment of awareness, say, of a finger touching something warm, your friend's hand. You have the experience of warmth. This warmth is just 'there'; but it is there in the setting of your consciousness of it being connected to your friend. It is there as a phenomenon in experience, and it has inherent significance for experience. The German language constructively refers to *Erlebnis*, lived experience, expressing the intrinsic bond between a phenomenon occurring and the phenomenon constituting part of a life. Phenomenologists examine the nature or structure of lived experience, and, very importantly, this involves radically rejecting imagery alluding to an observer 'in there', inside a person, looking at a world 'out there'. A reflective observer 'in there' reflecting on itself and, knowing that it reflects, would need to presuppose an observer observing the observer ... in infinite regress. In order to avoid this, phenomenologists argue, there has to be a 'ground', a non-perspectival phenomenon, a phenomenon that is just 'given'. The presently significant claim, then, is that awareness of the body moving, even if in the form of non-conscious proprioception, as 'pre-reflexive bodily awareness', is absolutely central to this ground (Gallagher 2005, pp. 137–138; Thompson 2007, pp. 250–251).

Modern phenomenology began as a distinct tradition in philosophy with the work of Edmund Husserl during the first three decades of the twentieth century. The starting point was a critique of approaches to mental life which sought to translate philosophical questions (for instance, what can we know?) into psychological research (how do we know?). Philosophy, Husserl argued, had to find a new starting point in description of phenomena as they exist for the reflective subject (the human person), emptied of or distanced from presuppositions about what the phenomena represent. Thus, description of movement should concern itself not with what moves and how but with the phenomenal characteristics, the qualities of movement as a phenomenon different from other phenomena. Description of the difference between active and passive movement, for example, the difference between the feel of the hand moving to touch the other hand and the feel of the hand touched, thus (in reasoning) precedes talk about hands and what they are doing.

Husserl was emphatic that the phenomenological character of something, the given fact, has *embodied* character. This is evident, for example, in the language he used to describe action and resistance to it at the base of an un-premeditated cognition: 'An object is constituted originally through spontaneity. The spontaneity of the lowest level is the one of *grasping*' (Husserl 1989, p. 26). It seemed linguistically appropriate to refer to the elemental form of understanding as a movement, 'grasping'. Accordingly, Husserl 'turned' to knowledge of touch and kinaesthesia to analyse knowledge of the body and the body's place in cognition. 'The Body as such can be constituted originally only in tactuality and in everything that is localized with the sensation of touch, for example, warmth, coldness, pain, etc. Furthermore, the kinaesthetic sensations play an important role' (Husserl 1989, p. 158). In one course of lectures, in 1907, Husserl attended to the character of the lived world as it concerns time and space, where he introduced the term kinaesthesia (Husserl 1997, p. 136). He implied that the term was previously not used in German, and he said he chose it because it permitted a discussion of the body as a moving body free from psychological implications and devoted to philosophical issues. (This is ironic, since precisely at this time, in English usage, the word flourished as a psychological term.) In this way, Husserl engaged with debate about the nature of the sense of movement and ensured it a place in phenomenological analysis.

There is a complication here. Husserl's project was a philosophical one: his concern was with the conditions of possibility for knowledge, say of space, not with the psychological how of space perception. But what he wrote appears almost continuously to move between the two registers, or levels, of inquiry – philosophical and psychological. (His lectures on philosophy exhibit a commanding knowledge of psychological research.) This practice in two registers has been and still is a noteworthy feature of phenomenological writing, even while the proper relations of philosophical and psychological knowledge remain in dispute.

The reader, I think, will find it hard to keep apart philosophy and psychology in the most influential of all of the scholars indebted to Husserl to write about perception, Maurice Merleau-Ponty.

Among Husserl's many manuscripts was a long essay, subsequently published under the English title, *Ideas Pertaining to a Pure Phenomenology and to a Phenomenological Philosophy. Second Book*, which the young French philosopher read closely just before the outbreak of World War II. Then, in 1945, Merleau-Ponty published *Phenomenology of Perception*. This has become the repeatedly cited, classic presentation of perception – the world we know, or cognize, through sensation, including sensation of our own bodies – as embodied activity. In considerable detail, Merleau-Ponty analysed the life of the senses, including the life of what he called sensed *motilité*, as that life appears to a conscious subject. This life, he constantly stressed, is embodied life with spatial, dynamic and temporal dimensions, tied in with sexuality, expression and speech and, not least, touch in all its forms.

Though Merleau-Ponty drew attention to the embodied nature of perception, he had little specific to say about a sense of movement. Sheets-Johnstone, in a major study, *The Primacy of Movement*, made this point. She is among a number of scholars who, in different ways, have linked what consciousness reveals about kinaesthesia and sensed movement to the biological place of sensed movement in the life of organisms. She integrated philosophical statements and psychological facts, as a result of which she treated movement as 'the ground' of being, 'an absolute', present as a condition of perception.

> In effect, what is already there ... is not the world and the body. What is already there is movement, movement, in and through which the perceptible world and acting subject come to be constituted, which is to say movement in and through which we make sense of both the world and ourselves. (Sheets-Johnstone 2011, p. 119)

There is no mind observing or perceiving body, this affirms, but rather action in the lived world in the course of the human organism's management of its social and physical environment. For ordinary speech, which confuses the philosophical and the psychological registers – or, perhaps it is more correct to say, rightly intuits their intimate relationship – this lived world is a world of movement. Examining the feel or phenomenal character of movement then prompts the question, whether this character of movement is intrinsic to the kinaesthetic sense or is the outcome of a change of spatial-temporal relations? That is, do we feel movement as movement or because one thing follows another and we call the relationship between the two things movement? Henri Bergson for one held the former view. He was:

> assured of the reality of the movement when it appears to me, within me, as a change of *state* or of *quality* ... The passage from one to another is also an absolutely real phenomenon. I hold then the two ends of the chain, muscular sensations within me, the sensible qualities of matter without me, and neither in the one case nor in the other do I see movement, if there be movement, as a mere relation: it is an absolute. (Bergson 2004, p. 258)

The research in the first half of the twentieth century of the gestalt psychologists and of the Belgian experimental psychologist, Albert Michotte, on the perception of causality tended to support this position. Michotte argued that we perceive cause flowing into effect rather than a sequence in which effect follows cause; we see a temporal process not one thing (cause) and then another thing (effect) (Michotte 1963). The perceptual world, the argument goes, has a ground in relational processes taking place in time, exemplified in phenomenal awareness of movement.

Phenomenological analysis and scientific inquiry into neural mechanisms are different undertakings. Berthoz and Petit, however, are among an impressive number of researchers to have argued that the two kinds of inquiry have to be brought into constructive relation if there is to be understanding of reflective life (Noë 2007; Berthoz and Petit 2008; Gallagher and Zahavi 2021). The argument is not just for dialogue but for the integration of (philosophical) practices in phenomenology, (biological) practices in the neurosciences and psychology. Much ongoing argument about this takes place under the auspices of research on *embodied cognition*. (Cognition, in this usage, denotes the engaged psychological relations between person and world as a whole, not only thinking.) While this is not the place either to review the debates or to claim new results, it is possible to explore relevant implications. Studies of embodied cognition first and foremost redirect standard cognitive science by taking up three themes, 'conceptualization', 'replacement' and 'constitution': 'the concepts on which an organism relies to understand its surrounding world depend on the kind of body that it has'; 'an organism's body in interaction with its environment replaces the need for representational processes thought to have been at the core of cognition'; and 'the body or world plays a constitutive rather than merely causal role in cognitive processing' (Shapiro 2011, p. 4). The claim is that the nature of the particular kind of body humans have, and the particular social worlds of bodies, shape the way thinking takes place, and the perceptions (always informed by emotions) that go into thinking can be better understood as actions rather than as representations, or sensory images or ideas.

The concept of *action* has a crucial bridging position in work linking phenomenological and experimental approaches. Psychologists writing on embodied cognition understand mental processes as actions, rather than brain functions, and recognize that actions involve sensed movement. Writing about perception, Alva Noë thus stated: 'to be a perceiver is to understand, implicitly, the effects of movement on sensory stimulation' (Noë 2004, p. 1). Regarding a perception as an activity, not a passive receptivity, leads to appreciation of the contribution of kinaesthesia to perception in general: the character of a sensation in experience is not intrinsic but related to the experience of an organism as it moves. Psychologists like Gibson had earlier pointed in this direction, emphasizing that perception is not a passive process, like mirroring, but an active one, like sculpting: what people do shapes what they perceive.

The imagery of experience consisting of an 'inner' observer 'looking out' is closely associated with Descartes, who divided the creation into matter stuff and mind stuff and, defining the two kinds of stuff in mutually exclusive terms, gave himself and subsequent generations the problem of saying how the two kinds of stuff could relate. The new science of the seventeenth century took on board the imagery of scientists as rational, experimental mirrors of nature (to adopt a figure of speech the philosopher Richard Rorty criticized in depth in *Philosophy and the Mirror of Nature*). Modern philosophy thereby became preoccupied with attempting to say how knowledge represents nature. For phenomenologists, this is all misguided. The objection is that there is no separate mind stuff and matter stuff, and there is no observer sitting inside the body using one kind of stuff to acquire knowledge of the other. Rather, the argument goes, there are processes, patterns of relations, brought about by actions. The feel of movement in particular and perception in general involve the relation, action-resistance, rather than a view in a mirror. Phenomenological descriptions do not refer phenomena to mind or body but to 'the lived world', and as such they have been attractive to writers concerned with 'the sense of life'. (This matters a lot in the world of dance.) Such descriptions, following Husserl's example, recognize the mental world as a world of 'value-Objects', that is a world having content with evaluative character, with worth (Husserl 1989, p. 29).

Recent writers on phenomenology and psychology, working within the framework of the theory of embodied cognition, have argued that what they variously call kinaesthesia and proprioception is essential for cognition in which an embodied subject manages its world and in the process knows itself. The master-key to the argument is the claim that 'perception [and cognition] is not something that happens to us, or in us. It is something we do' (Noë 2004, p. 1). As a consequence, embodied cognitivists argue, a purely passive subject would have no perceptual experience of an external world: movement is a condition of knowledge. This places action, rather than mental states or neural processes, at the centre of psychological inquiry. The scientist of the brain, Marc Jeannerod, wrote: the motor system is not 'an executive system that merely follows instructions elaborated somewhere else. Indeed, the motor system now stands as a probe that explores the external world, for interacting with other people and for gathering new knowledge' (Jeannerod 2006, p. vi). From this point of view, movement is the tool with which people explore the world. Those who live with young children would say the same. In this exploration, movement, giving rise to awareness of differences between kinaesthetic sensation and contact sensation plays a preponderant part in a person, perhaps a very young one, distinguishing between the body felt as owned, given in being human, and the bodies that are other to the perceiving subject. When there is movement, self and other differentiate. Kinaesthetic phenomena are at the centre of this.

It is commonplace to say that the mind thinks, or that, with lack of thought, fails to think. People used to say, 'that slipped my mind', though now I sometimes hear, 'that slipped my brain'. These are everyday expressions, but they are not accurate. An organism, human or animal, is engaged in doing what it does in living, and aspects of that doing involve it in thinking. The thinking is *in the processes* of doing – *in* the relations that constitute a life, the relations of the organism-environment-social situation, the relations of action-resistance. It is *people* who think. For the purposes of analysis and manipulation, researchers abstract from this complex or network of relations in order to focus on one part of the system, such as the mind's intentions, the brain's neurons or the muscles' performance. This kind of abstraction was notably central to the early decades of artificial intelligence (AI) research, undertaken as if minds/brains functioned without bodies. In reaction to this, evident from the 1980s, scientists, like Francisco J. Varela, Evan Thompson and Eleanor Roth in their influential book on *The Embodied Mind* (1993), opened up embodied cognitive psychology. Embodied cognitivists do not to talk about processes taking place 'in' the mind or 'in' the brain but discuss processes as events in the world, that is, as *actions*. This step makes possible the tie-in with phenomenological language about the embodied life-world.

There are many debates among embodied cognitivists, as there are between these psychologists and other types of cognitivists and neuropsychologists. Researchers who argue that the relations – in the body, in the surrounding environment, in society – in which mental processes are embedded have causal consequences for the way thinking, or perception, or memory or other mental processes occur, adopt the *enactive* approach. The term points to knowledge that perception is 'a kind of *involvement* with or *entanglement* with situations and things', and, I would emphasize, a *movement* in relation to situations and things (Noë 2007, p. 235; Fuchs 2021, p. 16; Gallagher and Zahavi 2021, p. 125). Noë declared that 'only a creature with certain kinds of bodily skill – for example, a base familiarity with the sensory effects of eye or hand movements – could be a perceiver' (Noë 2004, p. 2). It is doing, he held, that 'enacts' a perception, and doing invokes feels of movement; such feels are part of the constitution of mental processes. 'It is not the intrinsic character of a sensory stimulation that fixes the character of experience; rather, it is the way sensory stimulation varies as a function of movement in relation to the environment that does the important work' (Noë 2009, p. 63). This identifies phenomenal awareness of movement, including kinaesthetic sentience, as intrinsic to the ground of perception. It would seem right to consider this grounding as an existential as well as a psychological condition.

It is worth stopping for a moment to recall that an emphasis on action had a notable place in Soviet psychology. In the years after 1945, the Marxist psychologist Aleksei Leontiev, seeking a unifying theory, reworked the descriptive terms of psychological life in the light of the action that this life serves. He and others dubbed this activity theory (Chaiklin 2019). While there is some controversy about the actual nature of Leontiev's relations with his colleague of the 1920s, Lev Vygotsky, both Leontiev and Vygotsky understood psychological action as socially and culturally embedded. They directed attention away from mind abstractly considered towards the manner in which mental processes, such as perception, serve activity in the human world. There are theoretical parallels with the direction of embodied cognitivism. But I am not aware, in this connection, that Russian activity theorists gave any special attention to the sense of movement.

Whatever the arguments in cognitive psychology, it is clear that there is some kind of awareness of self-activity very early on in a child's life. This awareness, it appears, originates with the earliest proprioception:

> infants are in possession of proprioceptive information from birth ... and proprioception is 'the modality of the self par excellence'... It is through their early explorations of their own bodies that infants specify themselves as differentiated agents in the environment, eventually developing a more explicit awareness of themselves. (Gallagher and Zahavi 2021, p. 241, quoting Rochat 2001, p. 35)

Such views are of a piece with arguments made a century earlier, arguments which placed activity and kinaesthesia at the centre of cognition. In the words of John Dewey: 'I believe that the active side precedes the passive in the development of the child nature; that expression comes before conscious impression; that the muscular development precedes the sensory; that movements come before conscious sensations' (Dewey 2015, p. 228). Gallagher, among other scientists, has elaborated this argument in contemporary terms, identifying the formative place of proprioception in shaping the mental world.

> Movement and the registration of that movement in a developing proprioceptive system (that is, a system that registers its own self-movement) contributes to the self-organizing development of neuronal structures responsible not only for motor action, but for the way we come to be conscious of ourselves, to communicate with others, and to live in the surrounding world. Across the Cartesian divide, movement prefigures the links of intentionality, gesture formulates the contours of social cognition, and in both the most general and most specific ways, embodiment shapes the mind. (Gallagher 2005, p. 1)

The proprioceptive system is central both for the control of movement and for the shaping of the self-awareness fundamental to human relations. What goes on in a child's development is not the action of mind or events in body but, rather, movement, which gives the child the contours of being a person in possession of the capacities of cognition and gesture.

An individual's development cannot be understood in terms of separate states of mind and body somehow influencing each other, though development manifestly occurs in and through bodies. There are neuronal events, which require investigation with special techniques (for which we have the natural sciences), and there are intentions, meanings and values, the investigation of which requires quite other methods (for which we have the humanities and social sciences). However, ordinary language accounting for what people do does not follow this division. Nor do the arguments of the psychologists advancing theories of embodied cognition and advocating the notion of organisms, including humans as first and foremost actors, embodied participants moving in embodied biological and social worlds. From the viewpoint taken in these arguments, references to mind events or brain events (or what is said to go on 'in the mind' or 'in the brain') denote actions, interventions, responses to affordances in the human organism's relations with the surroundings, practices in carrying out a life.

Animals and humans need brains to do what they do, but they do what they do as animals and people, not as brains. To make the point, I mention research on mirror neurons. Everybody knows that imitation of movements is common (your companion yawns, and you follow suit), and that when you see from a facial expression (which is also a movement) someone reveal an emotion, you may feel a similar emotion and/or make a similar expression (or movement). Neuroscientists have suggested that the same neurons are active in the initiator and in the imitator, and they have claimed to have discovered localized sites of such neurons, 'mirror neurons', in the brain. Some enthusiasts then interpreted this as the discovery of a natural basis for empathy in the brain: my neurons naturally mirror yours, and so I will naturally feel as you feel. Researchers into performance extended the approach to the appreciation of dance: the viewer's brain is activated in a similar manner to a performer's, and the viewer feels the pleasures and pains of dance movement. There are problems with the approach, however. For a start empirical knowledge of localized mirror neurons is not clear-cut. More relevant for present purposes is an old point: there is much more to the social activity of watching movement or dancing than the firing of particular neural systems in the brain. It is not possible to reduce the social relations of people, or of performers and their audiences, to the activity of mirror neurons (even if in fact they do form a distinct system). We need language that relates people to people, people as social actors to other social actors. There is also strong argument that when people share actions and emotions they share because they inhabit and participate in the same world, not necessarily because they imitate each other.

The importance of proprioception in life is confirmed by clinical evidence, and one case in particular has been much discussed. There is a fortunately exceedingly rare medical condition in which a person loses all tactile and proprioceptive capacity below the head. (Were *all* the capacity lost, presumably the person would be completely inert or dead.) Accounts of Ian Waterman's brave and determined life have made this condition relatively well known. Following an illness when he was nineteen, Waterman lost touch and movement below the neck. There was no damage to the motor nervous system but loss in the tactile and proprioceptive sensory system. Working with Jonathan Cole, a clinical neurophysiologist, he learned to report on what he could and could not feel. He could feel temperature and pain, for instance. He learned to work around his condition, to move and to walk: his life thus turned out to be one extended experiment, through its absence, in the place of proprioception.

> Every movement is planned in advance, the force and direction calculated intuitively, and the movement monitored [visually] as it is taking place. Given all these requirements, it is impressive to see IW move without visible flaw at normal speeds. Although his gait seems somewhat lumbering (he calls it controlled falling), his arm and hand movements are truly indistinguishable from normal. However, if vision is denied, IW can no longer control his hands and arms accurately. (McNeill et al. 2008, p. 2)

The effects of severe strokes offer parallels to this life (and recall the case Bell reported, of the woman who could not hold her baby unless she looked at it). Damage to movement may come with loss of sensory as well as motor functions. Therapy, therefore, works with sensory as well as motor activity, as part of one system. The phantom limb phenomenon, in which a person perceives the presence and movement of a limb when, after accident or amputation, it is not there, vividly brings home the importance of proprioception to all of this. As the developmental psychologist Philippe Rochat observed, 'the proprioception of our own body is so ingrained that adult and even child amputees commonly perceive phantom limbs' (Rochat 2001, p. 35).

The 'ingrained' nature of proprioception underlies Feldenkrais Method and other movement and posture therapies, like Alexander Technique. Feldenkrais practitioners use relaxation, suggestion and movement to encourage patients to be consciously aware of and reflective about kinaesthetic sensation, and this may involve bringing proprioceptive sensory impulses into awareness. They use very slow and gentle manipulations, or the patient's own actions or even simply rest, to achieve change. This involves a kind of training of a person's body in self-awareness, and the techniques can be used with very young children. The purpose is to use awareness (though it may, as proprioceptive awareness, be non-conscious) to enhance the ability to adapt to what the body can and cannot do. Here there is an interesting tie-up with an abstract point in Husserl's analysis, repeated by Merleau-Ponty. According to these authors, the structure of consciousness in thought is better formulated as 'I can' rather than as 'I think that', meaning that a cognitive event (technically, its intentionality) is a kinaesthetically informed action rather than a representation (Husserl 1989, pp. 266–277; Thompson 2007, pp. 313–314).

Research in phenomenology and in cognitive psychology has thus come together in an emphatic focus on the embodied mind which necessarily invokes analysis of kinaesthesia and proprioception. As the word 'embodied' does a lot of work, and as this intensifies interest in kinaesthetic processes, it will be helpful to enlarge perspective in another way, by asking why 'embodied' is a buzz-word of contemporary culture. There are a number of possible explanations for the word's ubiquity, and I suggest three. (Perhaps some psychologists would attribute the spread simply to the progress of science.)

The first point is straightforward. Early computer science and AI research concentrated on the challenges of hardware and software development, and in the process the research often totally ignored the fact that it is humans with bodies in social environments who think and act with intelligence. Scientists themselves perceived this limitation and, from the 1980s, they began systematically to take on board the complexities of actual cognition, meaning that they began to acknowledge that brains do not sit in vats (as a much used image in philosophical discussion expresses it) and that people not brains act in the world. As a result, 'the notion of embodiment, the notion of an embodied mind or a minded body, is meant to replace the ordinary notions of mind and body, both of which are derivations and abstractions' (Gallagher and Zahavi 2021, p. 151). This also led to the argument that brains cannot literally be computers (however much computers may model aspects of their working), since brains live in the bodies of sociable people and computers do not. The game-changing step was to declare the embodied nature of brains and cognition. In this context, the word 'embodied' signalled 'the move' of scientists and fellow-travellers out of the narrow disciplinary and theoretical confines of AI research. The benefits have been enormous. Not least, there is now a very considerable body of research on the way the emotions profoundly inform cognition (Boddice and Smith 2020;

Fuchs and Koch 2014). Though it might be thought that no ordinary person would ever have doubted this, earlier AI researchers had ignored it.

Other reasons for the ubiquitous adoption of the word 'embodiment' originate with changes in the surrounding culture. There is a long and noble tradition tracing the activity of reason back to Ancient Greece; for many Europeans this tradition is the glory of European civilization. It seems right to conclude, however, that the barbarism of the twentieth and twenty-first centuries, along with a deep reassessment of the history of slavery, colonialism and the exercise of power between different human groups, such as the power men have exercised over women, has led to a devaluing, or a down-grading, of the status of 'the European mind'. I am far from alone in taking such a view. Lloyd, with a comparative view of ancient Greek and Chinese science in mind, wrote:

> With the events of the twentieth century still vivid in our memories, we can certainly not say that we are saner human beings, better able to organize our affairs, than those who used be looked down on as archaic or primitive, Nor has the twenty-first century begun exactly auspiciously. (Lloyd 2012, p. 2)

Viewed against the background of this judgment, thought about the embodied character of mind appears part of the break-out from confidence in the super-rational European intellect. Put baldly, the earlier faith in reason appears misguided, because it was not faith in embodied reason. The language of embodiment appears to be language appropriate for the actualities of the world, unlike the language of idealized abstraction produced by earlier educated, white and mostly male elites. It is always possible to find quotations to bolster this reaction. Montero, discussing the aesthetic senses, cited the Harvard University philosopher George Santayana on perceiving beauty: 'the soul ... is glad to forget its connection with the body' (Montero 2006, p. 232). This, by contemporary Western standards, is an astounding remark.

This viewpoint is especially sharp in higher education. Higher education was long associated with training the mind, principally through the Classics and mathematics, of a class of people whose occupation would be mental work and governing others. People whose occupation depended on manual labour were either unskilled or, if skilled, trained by apprenticeship, not formal education, and they occupied lower positions in social hierarchies. The current emphasis on the embodied nature of even mental work challenges these old, and still persisting, hierarchies. The dance scholar and performer, Susan Leigh Foster, directly attributed the lack of attention to kinaesthesia to scholarly scorn for the body:

> Pervasive mistrust of the body, and the classification of its information as either sexual, unknowable, or indecipherable, have resulted in a paucity of activities that promote awareness of the body's position and motion, or the degree of tension in its muscles. (Foster 2011, p. 7)

The challenge is visible in the widening of the scope of universities to include all kinds of training (in soldiering, in art performance and in the manufacture of agricultural machinery, for instance). This in turn has brought with it 'moves' to examine students by practice rather than through written work – examination by embodied work rather than written, disembodied reason. Thus, there is a lot at stake on embodiment as a notion in the world of higher education.

A further reason for the spread of references to embodiment lies in political economy. As the figure of speech, 'it's all in the mind', implies, there are many occasions when the life of the mind is judged to be vague, idiosyncratic and impractical – not part of 'the real world'. It is implied, in contrast, that the life of the body is concrete, shared and real. It may be a liberating judgment, liberating individuals of whatever ethnic origin, social background, gender and education to assert the value, expressed through the body, of their preferred way of life. This kind of liberation has been evident, for instance, in popular dance. On the other hand, turning everything that matters into dimensions of bodily life recreates all aspects of being human as material objects which can be bought and sold, manufactured and marketed, that is, owned and manipulated by institutions with power and capital. To be sure, ancient economies included clothing and cosmetics embellishing the body; but economies now encompass rebuilding bodies with prosthetics, gene banks, pharmaceuticals and all kinds of surgery and devices which many people feel as extensions of themselves. If everything human is embodied, it would seem, everything human is a marketable product. The widespread emphasis on embodiment may be a sign of just how far this historical process has already gone.

Leaving further comments on social change to the discussion of agency, I return to the nature of the sense of movement. Wider perspectives will have more precision with a better appreciation of this sense and the place of kinaesthesia within movement.

6 Movement and time

Movement takes place *in time* as well as in space; there is temporal as well as spatial navigation. The descriptive science of the mechanics of movement, kinematics, relates variables of time and space, and the descriptive science of awareness of movement must do the same. However time is conceived, whether, following Kant, as an a priori condition of experience, or as the product of activity, there can be no motion and no feeling of motion outside of time.

The sensory world has sequential (diachronic) as well simultaneous (synchronic) form: we see a dance movement or hear a melody unfold in time: 'Any movement ... we perceive is embedded in a temporal horizon' (Gallagher and Zahavi 2021, p. 81). Philosophers and psychologists disagree about whether the temporal nature of sensory awareness can be analysed in terms of separate slices of time, like the individual frames of a film, or whether sensory awareness is intrinsically spread over time. Awareness of movement adds weight to the argument that the sensory world is in its nature temporal, that is, has duration, or, as James expressed it, exists as a 'stream of thought' – in a stream, there is a continuous 'flow' (James 1950, vol. I, p. 279; contemporaries of James said something similar). It is not possible to conceive of movement in a timeless instant; indeed, one might even say, suggestively, that a sense of movement *is* a sense of time. (The phrase, 'a sense of time', refers to yet another human 'sense'.)

Taking a broad view, it may be said that over the centuries inquirers into perception have had three orientations. There have been those who think the sensory world is built up from sensory units coming together (in a process called association) in time and space, like building blocks assembling themselves; there have been those who think this too but believe the building requires an active mind, existing independently of and prior to sensations in order to carry out the

DOI: 10.4324/9781003368021-8

assembly; and there are those who have argued that the unification is built into the content of sensory processes. Locke exemplifies the first position, Kant the second and gestalt psychologists the third. Though the discussion is most often about vision, analysis of the kinaesthetic sense has much to contribute and supports the third orientation. Movement is felt as a whole and not as a sequence of stages or a construction – hence the appositeness of metaphors of flow and streams. A driver feels a hand moving to grasp the gear-lever, not a sequence of positions. Here experimental studies of visual perception of movement of objects and of the perception of causal relations between physical things are relevant. Studies indicate that the change evident to consciousness in a movement or in a causal process is given in the sensory world; it is a feature of sensory activity not centrally constructed by mind or brain. (Michotte carried out refined experimental studies to support this view of perception of causal relations.) If this is so, then the sense of movement may indeed be fundamental for the sense of time: the sense 'comes with' temporal awareness built into its nature.

The subjective feel of movement is ephemeral: it happens, and then it is over. There is no lasting subjective representation, though of course it is possible to have a memory of subjective movement or to make a record of objective movement in which the memory or record (like a film) also takes place in time. In English there is repeatedly reference to time 'passing', and this strikingly differentiates description of knowledge of movement in time from knowledge of movement in space, since space does not 'pass'. A self-movement over time has a different character in consciousness from that of objective movement measured in the spatial world. Sheets-Johnstone therefore concluded:

> Self-movement does not show itself in ways other than the way it is. And that way is moreover ephemeral, not enduring. Obviously something quite different is going on in the perception and constitution of self-movement than in the perception and constitution of objects in the world. (Sheets-Johnstone 2011, p. 132)

With these points in mind, it is a natural, if speculative, step to suggest that the sense of movement, which in some form develops early in the pre-natal child, substantially and, it may be, essentially contributes to the sense of time. The hypothesis is that the early, perhaps earliest, patterns of sensations establish the order in subjective awareness that is described as time 'passing'. The relevant early patterns of sensation come with the foetus's action and with resistance to that action, and with sensation of the rhythmic vibratory movements of the mother's heartbeat and breathing. Rhythm, in its nature temporal, which has a 'pre-reflective' place in adult perception (as in foot-tapping), may be a very elemental component of the sensed temporal world. The comparison, or even identification, of sensed movement with sensed time, requires some comment on understandings of time. In natural science, exemplified in formal mechanics, time is the measurable fourth dimension, additional to the three dimensions of space. The general theory of relativity fully integrated the time dimension into cosmology and accounts of the physical world, and the power of analysis of time as a fourth dimension has been amply demonstrated. The mathematics of the calculus supplied a tool for handling the continuously varying change that time introduces into mechanics; indeed, when invented in the late seventeenth century, it was known as the theory of 'fluxions', with definite connotations of movement. Nevertheless, in spite of this history of science, there is a significant body of philosophical work which judges it wrong to treat time as if it were a dimension comparable to the dimensions of space and measurable in ways comparable to space. The core of the objection is the intuition that time 'passes', that there is an inherently qualitative mode to time. In phenomenal awareness, time exists as qualitative *duration*. The model for thinking about time in this way comes from the life cycle, from birth, growth and death, not from changes in spatial relations.

The life cycle is also the template of live artistic performance. Performances start up, or are 'born', they pass through the world 'flaring-up' or 'flowering' and they 'die' (or 'die down'); like life, they come and they go. This may be a central piece in the puzzle about why live performance matters: live performance ends and cannot be repeated (though of course it may be recorded), and the temporality of this, generating tension and excitement that the instant is unrepeatable, is all or nothing and will soon be over, is of utmost importance to performers and audiences alike. We do not live twice but perform on the world's stage only once. The same argument may explain the aesthetic value of an original work of art compared with a copy or fake (however good): the original has a history that 'passed' only once, and it is the fact that that passing moment has gone that gives value (Lem 2013, p. 226). Music for its part is inherently temporal, and for this reason we divide music into 'movements'.

The best known philosophical argument to reject all theories comparing the temporal dimension to spatial dimensions is in Bergson's *Essai sur les données immédiates de la conscience* ('Essay on the immediate givens of consciousness', 1913). The French title

(and English sub-title) conjures up associations with the phenomenology of time consciousness. This is appropriate because Bergson
drew on what he claimed to be the direct evidence of the conscious
world and concluded that time is lived duration, qualitative change,
not in its nature, or essence, measurable except for abstract purposes
that detract from its reality. Bergson was well informed about the
debate on the nature of the muscular sense, and he supported the
view that there is some kind of centrally originating awareness of
action (in this, following Maine de Biran). But because of his critique
of treatments of time as a dimension analogous to dimensions of
space, he did not argue for a psychological theory of developing
awareness of time based on an elementary sense of movement. Time,
for Bergson, was not derived, but given, intuited, in awareness.

Despite Bergson's critique, psychology and everyday imagination
in Western cultures has largely continued to relate perception of
space and perception of time. The position Bergson opposed was
clearly present in a statement by his contemporary, the philosopher
and poet Jean-Marie Guyau, who wrote: 'It is movement in space
which creates time in human consciousness. Without movement
there is no time' (quoted in Wearden 2016, p. 7). As Guyau's words
suggest, it appears natural to link what is said about space to what is
said about time. Even James, who both knew Bergson and spread the
imagery of time flowing, included visual diagrams in his discussion of
time, making evident the spatial character of his imagination on the
topic.

The phenomenologists set out to analyse time, as they analysed
any other aspect of the phenomenal world, as it is, without presumptions about its essential nature. They asked, so to say, how time
feels, and in answering they drew on the sense of movement. As I
have asserted, a person feels movement, not one state followed by
another, just as a person hears a melody. Movement is sensed as
extended in time and is more like a flow than a succession of states, a
flow 'carrying over' from the immediate past, through the present,
into the immediate future (the retentional, present and protentional
elements of Husserl's analysis). Husserl declared that consciousness
must 'encompass more than what is given right now – it must be
co-conscious of what has just been, and what is just about to occur'
(in the words of Gallagher and Zahavi 2021, p. 79). Merleau-Ponty
made the same claim:

> Each present permanently underpins a point of time which calls
> for recognition from all the others, so that the object is seen at all

times as it is seen from all directions and by the same means, namely the structure imposed by a horizon. (Merleau-Ponty 2002, pp. 79–80)

The temporal dimension also fundamentally matters in the integration of the kinaesthetic and proprioceptive elements essential for performance. This is made strikingly visible in the clinical condition called motion agnosia, in which a patient sees the world freezing in place, unmoving for several seconds, before it is suddenly arranged in a new position. The break in temporal continuity badly disrupts action.

The degree to which a moving person is aware of the temporal horizon is, however, highly variable. Certainly, it is often not conscious, and writing on felt movement is rather unusual. All the same, the mountaineer Reinhold Messner, for one, left a memorable description of 'flow':

> Climbing is like ballet. Every second of the performance is different, as the structure of the rock determines how I compose and choreograph the moves. When I'm climbing well, I'm not thinking at all. It's all instinctive, and if I find the right flow, the climbing just happens of its own accord. It's as if gravity has been abolished. (Messner 2014, p. 45)

This description links movement in space and time, and the link is evaluative ('the right flow'). This, I suggest, points to the qualitative significance that movement, conceived as duration, has in any performance involving movement, whether climbing, dance or just walking along. It also draws attention to the emotional or affective character of sensed movement, as indeed everyday language does when referring to the good or bad timing of an action.

The phenomenology of time, elaborated in *Being and Time* (1927), is central to Heidegger's philosophical reputation. In this respect like Bergson (but only in this respect), Heidegger analysed time as a condition of a human being the kind of being a human is, not as a dimension comparable to spatial dimensions. Though his work was in fundamental philosophy and did not concern itself with psychology, it re-enforced two elements which matter to psychological discussion. Firstly, understanding the human person as being-in the world, he analysed an existential condition of inherently embodied being. Secondly, he upheld the argument that knowledge of the world is given, not derived: we are *in the world* – there is no inner observer of an outer world. Further, in passing, Heidegger noted that the sense of reality may well develop through resistance to action; he did not, however, go into the facts that might support or oppose such a view (as Husserl had done) (Heidegger 1967, p. 254). In ordinary speech, it is possible to say that a person develops a feel for reality. Strictly speaking, though, reality (as opposed to a feel for reality) denotes a philosophical concept, and in Heidegger's philosophical judgment reality is given in being. The being of being human has death as the horizon in relation to which humans experience time. It is, therefore, human finitude that is, in the final analysis, the temporal horizon in relation to which any movement has meaning or significance. Not coincidentally, Heidegger and other phenomenologists wrote about being human as a condition of being 'thrown' into the world: it is not of our choosing we are here, and the condition we are in is likened to a movement carried out on us.

There is a considerable body of experimental work on time perception separate from phenomenological analysis. Much focuses on judgment of time intervals and the way it is affected by factors like emotion and aging (Wearden 2016). There is also extensive work on memory. Beyond noting that it is abundantly clear that many elements contribute to time perception, there is no call to go into the issues here.

Both sensed movement and music unfold in time. Since 'it is hard to deny the conviction that there is a way music moves that we can imitate with the movement of our bodies', there has been much relevant research on music, melody and rhythm. Moreover, 'music is closely tied to time, which it structures, and since time is experienced as moving, so is music' (Carroll and Moore 2008, pp. 414, 418). The experience of rhythm 'pulsating' and melody 'flowing' suggests intimate links between proprioceptive processes and sound. It has therefore been suggested that 'the movement in the dance [to music] clarifies, enlarges, or expands upon the feelings of movement already available in the pertinent sort of music' (Carroll and Moore 2008, p. 415). Numerous forms of bodily exercise and training rely on the intimacy of heard and felt rhythm, leading experimental psychologists to explore the common processes at work. Already in the 1880s, the Berlin psychologist Carl Stumpf had concluded that 'it looks, indeed, as if our sense of rhythm and time was essentially developed in connection with the movements of locomotion' (quoted in Ruckmich 1913, p. 308). Also beginning in the 1880s, Émile Jaques-Dalcroze developed eurhythmics as a form of musical training specifically through movement. Many forms of gymnastics and exercises have followed suit. So do traditions of prayer, as in the rocking movements accompanying Orthodox Jewish prayer, or the chanted liturgy in traditions originating in the early Christian churches.

Writing about the human upright posture, Straus noted: 'it is not poetry alone that moves on "metrical feet" in an anapaestic, iambic or trochaic meter. In marching, in dancing, we perform a great variety of set patterns' (Straus 1952, p. 543). He also referred to breathing and walking as 'a continuously arrested falling' (Straus 1952, p. 542) and believed that these movements are the evolutionary and developmental base of not just awareness of rhythm but of awareness of time, conceived as having extension or duration. Sheets-Johnstone argued:

> We constitute space and time originally in our kinesthetic consciousness of movement. Flux, flow, a streaming present, a stream of thought, consciousness, or subjective life, a style of change – all such descriptive terms are in both a temporal and spatial sense rooted in originary self-movement: they are all primordially present not in the constitution of objects but in our original spontaneity of self-movement, in our original experience and sense of our dynamically moving bodies. (Sheets-Johnstone 2011, p. 159)

Such insights also contribute to an understanding of why the link between biological rhythms and time, vibratory movements and energy all fed into the modernist arts of the early twentieth century (Reynolds 2007). It is also possible to find parallels in post-modernist and avant-garde performance in which artists have used the transitory nature of movement to create an aesthetics of the ephemeral: if everything moves, nothing endures. An illustration comes with the dancer's interest in falling. Falling, of course, is precisely the form of movement dancers generally strive to avoid as an intensely unwelcome interruption in flow. Yet, there is a contemporary interest in both the techniques of falling – even of throwing oneself to the ground – and the metaphor of falling, whether to demonstrate collapse or to demonstrate the positive expression that can come out of the initially unexpected and unwanted. 'As mind and body interact so vibrantly, a practice of intentional falling – surrendering to gravity to be supported by the ground – releases fluidity of thought and provides physical resources for living with psychological uncertainty' (Claid 2021, p. 2). Use of the fall becomes a way to interrupt time and to start again. If, with Heidegger, we imagine the human situation as being 'thrown' into a world not of human choosing, the fall introduced into performance may be seen as a way to imagine choice.

This brief discussion of time brings to a close the more directly philosophical and scientific side of these perspectives on kinaesthesia and the feel of movement. I now want to put the perspectives to work and interpret what is going on in the cultural life of movement. Nietzsche wrote: '*Sit* as little as possible; give no evidence to any thought that was not born while one moved about freely – in which the muscles are not celebrating a feast too. All prejudices come from the intestines' (Nietzsche 1969b, pp. 239–240). This is relevant rhetoric in the age of keyboards and Zoom.

Part III

Third movement: minuet and trio

7 Free dance

Imagine that you are watching a performance in a 'black box'. Some readers will be familiar with this, but others not. The box in question is a dance space with no stage, a kind of large studio, a plain space, sometimes with seating on a level with or around the dance floor. The space is functional, and the dark walls maximize the visibility of movement in light. It is space for contemporary dance, which as modern dance, opposing the rules of ballet and free from the patterns of ritual dance, in the early twentieth century opened up new bodily movements as an art form. It turned out to be a form without boundaries. One or more dancers move in the space in the black box, characteristically with dramatic energy and youthful flexibility. The movement may be abstract, it may articulate a plot, and it may express an existential condition or a political emotion. There is highly varied and often experimental use of lighting, music, computing technology and video. Perhaps one dancer is zapping about the floor in a wheel chair; perhaps another dancer is moving with and then detaching an artificial limb; perhaps a professional dancer and a person with Down's syndrome are moving together. Contemporary dance movement varies enormously and voices a great range of social, gendered and political identity. But what goes on, and what the space of the box highlights, is movement.

Dance studies covering all forms of dance are well aware of the intimate relation between 'outward' movement and its 'inner' feel, the kinaesthetic world (using the term in its broad meaning). It is unusual, however, for the feel of movement itself to be the primary focus of attention. (For an influential exception, Foster 2011.) Nevertheless, put at its simplest, I suggest that dance is the everyday appreciation of movement as life writ large. In dance, the subjective world of being a living person becomes the objective world of an art form. Sheets-Johnstone wrote: 'At their most fundamental level,

DOI: 10.4324/9781003368021-10

subjective experiences are tactile-kinesthetic experiences. They are experiences of one's own body and body movement; they are experiences of animate form' (Sheets-Johnstone 2011, p. 376). The 'animate form' of dance creates a shared bodily life for the subjective world. It recreates biological life as a vividly shared culture; it recreates culture in the body.

Art is not something apart from daily life, however much the classic models of art and the institutions – the art gallery, the concert hall, the theatre – which house or perform these models make it seem that way. The closeness of art and everyday life is especially clear in the arts of movement, since movement is what people do all the time (even in dreaming, eyes flicker). To bring home this point, in the middle of discussing dance I insert a trio which relates dance to walking. (Much of what there is to say relates also to sport, though this is largely left to one side.) Discussing walking in turn leads to consideration of people's relations to the immediate spatial and temporal world in which they live and move. In whatever mediated and elaborated forms they take, dance and walking establish *relations*. To adapt a current figure of speech, dance 'folds' life: the mundane surface of practical everyday movement, including walking, becomes the richly involuted, refracted and transformed folding of dance movements.

Free or modern dance began around 1900 in reaction to ballet, after the Russian choreographer Marius Petipa had created such lasting masterpieces as 'Swan Lake' and the classic revision of 'Coppélia'. Women featured prominently among the innovators, and their free movement was about dress, public presence and independence in way of life as well as about art. The interwoven life and performance of the American dancer, Isadora Duncan, is exemplary: she titled her autobiographical manifesto, 'The Dance of the Future', and she even set up a dance school in revolutionary Russia to bring together the dance and the social future she thought then being forged. She took her model of ideal movement from what she saw on pottery and sculpture and imagined of the art of Ancient Greece. She thought the movement she saw embodied the dynamic harmony of the human body, the human soul and the natural world. She performed to classical music and aspired to dance natural movements, dancing bare-foot, moving her torso and using weight to give momentum. The contrast with ballet was blatant: flowing tunics and bare feet, not tights, shoes and bodices, visible weight not the illusion of weightlessness, the flow of music not a sentimental story line. During her early years, her innovations simply stunned audiences, and she was embraced by the artistic avant-garde (Daly 1992; Franko 1995, chapter 1; S. Manning 1997). Dance has

Figure 7.1 Dancing couple (2006). Photograph, Tomasz Jaworski. Courtesy of Tomasz Jaworski. Copyright © Tomasz Jaworski.

now become so free that imagination is needed to recognize the impact she had. I therefore quote from the memoir of Stefanida Rudneva, who as a highly cultured young woman (she was seventeen) saw Duncan dance in Saint-Petersburg in December 1907.

> And, thus, I sit in the balcony of the old, inconvenient, long concert hall. In front of me the empty stage and hanging 'carpet and curtains', and from the corner comes out and goes along in front of the backdrop such a simple, such a quiet, such an unseen and familiar movement – not that 'leap from a Greek vase', not that move out from a Pompeian fresco – she halted, having finished her movement. Ah! – such a 'wounded Amazon'. The first impression ... 'the resurrection of ancient beauty, joy and truth'. And from this 'meeting' flow tears, and the heart freezes in rapture ...
>
> Such joy of life, creativity, giving to people, radiated from each of her movements, that the wish was born: 'I also want thus to dance ecstatically, so to live, to be such a joyful and authentic person'. (Rudneva 2007, p. 97)

Duncan's movement gave Rudneva direction in life. Rudneva went on to be a founding member of a small studio of musical movement, 'Heptachor', whose practitioners still continue the tradition she initiated and sustained.

Other innovators in movement generated similar excitement. Loïe Fuller, working within the tradition of music hall, used batons and fabrics to extend her arms into flowing wings, and Mary Wigman, indebted to theatre, developed expressive movements as dramatic gesture or mime (as in the celebrated '*Hexentanz*' – 'Witch dance', first performed in 1914) which bore the full range of emotion. With time, and with the establishment of studios to teach the new forms of movement, free dance instituted its own standards and traditions of movement, and the history and overcoming of these practices leads into the world of contemporary dance.

Martha Graham founded and directed her vastly influential school of modern dance in the interwar years. Distancing herself from the notion of dance as entertainment, she sought out the elemental components of movement. These she found in a stylized appreciation of breathing, leading to a technique in teaching dance based on contraction and release in the body, understood to be expressive of freeing or restricting emotions and of independence or dependence on gravity. She then added spiral motions to training to enhance fluidity of

Figure 7.2 'Light dances' (2011), Pavalon, Noyes School of Rhythm, Portland,
CT, USA. Dancer, Meg Brooker; photograph, Christopher Graefe.
Courtesy of Meg Brooker.

movement. A much quoted statement, 'movement never lies', reveals
the intensity of ideals in her practice (Graham 1992, p. 20). She in fact
wrote this as a report of an explanation given to her by her father, a
physician and specialist in nervous diseases. Her father was responding
to her questions as a girl when she was trying to understand the
withdrawn posture and silence of a visitor to their house, and her
father referred to symptoms of illness. The saying, however, has
acquired standing as a declaration of belief in the authenticity of the
body and its movements created in Graham's work and in the work of
many later dancers. In social worlds where public statements cannot be
trusted and when social actions are not what they are said to be,
Graham's words have come to say that the personal body remains
there as an authentic guide. The words are a clarion call to truth in the
language of movement.

Also early in the twentieth century, with independent roots but richly interacting with free dance, there were numerous innovations in popular dance. Beginning in the social worlds of Latin America and in communities of African Americans, the tango, the maxixe, animal dances and syncopated movement to jazz became the rage across the Americas and Europe. The dances transferred to bourgeois salons and cafes as ballroom. Then, after World War II, they transformed again and gave rise to contemporary rock and disco culture and TV and pop video routines. All this movement is now so taken for granted that it seems a direct expression of life. So much is this case that I want to draw a parallel, however distant and anecdotal it may at first seem. Once upon a time in the country at dawn, I watched two rabbits. They sat unmoving, resting back on their hind legs, facing the growing source of light beyond the horizon. When the first brilliant rays of the sun came over the field, the pair sprang into the air, ran around and – danced. A disco in full swing, a running child, a leaping animal ...

People show pleasure as they move and, in some circumstances, pain. The fact is, however, that people who make movement their purpose, especially professional movers – dancers, sports people, climbers, racing-car drivers, acrobats – do not talk much about the specific feeling of movement. They talk about technique, about motivation, about difficulties in achieving their goals, about routines or routes, but not so much about the sense of movement or kinaesthetic awareness. This is primarily because movement and the control of movement are to a large degree non-conscious events. Though the proprioception essential to activity is a sensory function, it is to a large extent outside awareness and taken for granted. The feel of movement is substantially tacit. Evidently, though, there is emotional pleasure in simply moving and in achieving harmonious or expressive movement. Dancers certainly note when a movement feels right or wrong. A dancer practising or exploring a movement will confidently and, as if intuitively, assert that the move is not quite right, or that, yes, this is the move or posture sought. This self-assessment does not depend on vision, on seeing movement or posture in a mirror, though this may contribute, but on the unmediated feel of movement. A contemporary dancer may well prefer to 'look within' rather than look in a mirror to work through a move. Non-dancers know a good deal about movement too, for example when they balance to find stability on a moving train or run down a staircase. Many people, seeing a fine runner or ballet dancer, find beauty in a performance efficiently or, as people say, effortlessly accomplished. There is also emotion and pleasure in stilling movement, as in relaxation or yoga, and there is displeasure in being required to stay still for too long. There is pain in excessive strain or suddenness of movement and also pain, or at least discomfort, in fatigue.

Appreciating dance as an art form, however, that is, appreciating it aesthetically, 'goes beyond' individual tacit knowledge and subjective pleasures and pains to shared social practices (Copeland and Cohen 1983). Practices hugely vary: the folk dance with a large place in sustaining local or national identity; the rave for release and rebellion from work; the contemporary dance piece exposing new forms of movement as avant-garde art; the political statement (I recall a video of a Russian girl, in tutu, on a snowy road at minus 15 degrees, pirouetting with manacled hands); the entertainment of 'Strictly Come Dancing' on BBC TV; the formal beauty of the ballet; the ritualistic performance of religious dances, such as the swirling dervishes of the Sufi faith. Faced by this variety, any general theory about why people dance, and why people watch dance, appears likely to founder. Nevertheless, dance scholars find meaning in particular instances. And, insofar as generalization is possible and desirable, it is going to have movement at the centre.

In order to illustrate the knowledge of the particularities of purpose and context required to say why people dance, I describe the movement practices G. I. Gurdjieff initiated and taught to his followers (Sirotkina and Smith 2017, chapter 5). Gurdjieff was of Armenian-Greek heritage, and like many others of his generation, living through urban transformation, World War I and the Russian Revolution, he sought to combine Western insight and Eastern practices to give modern people potential for a full life. He required a person 'to wake' to harmony of the mind, the body and the emotions. Seeking techniques 'to wake' his followers and lead them to attend to the powers inside themselves, he set up a teaching centre in which he required participation in both physical work and dance-like exercises. His technique depended on 'waking' to movement. He created a prototype of many other practices, such as those recently directed towards achieving mindfulness, which foster kinaesthetic awareness, awareness of movement and stillness, as a state transcending, or uniting, mind, body and emotion and restoring harmony in a person.

> Bringing a totality to our movements, our activities, we can suddenly realize that deep within, there is a still point, which does not know the world of efforts. It is the ground of our Being ...

Such is the inner process, the inner dance of attention, from the inner to the outer, from the outer to the inner. Learning to sense our body from inside, first one fragment after the other successively, then combining them, suddenly this sensation radiates to the whole of ourselves, a vivid sensation of existing as One. This experience can be called Presence. (Gurdjieff Dances, unpaginated)

The goal of the practice, of 'the inner dance of attention', is the achievement of 'Presence' or, it might be said in phenomenological language, being-for-itself. Not by chance, this notion of presence has also emerged as an ideal and is much discussed in performance studies (Macneill 2014, chapter 4). It is also a feature of religious thought: in the Christian tradition, the model of presence is transubstantiation, the miraculous presence of the body and blood of Christ at the culmination of the Mass. Analogously, in performance presence occurs when 'everything comes together' and there is an ecstatic moment, as when Pavlova, in the most famous of all performances of 'Swan Lake', 'really was' the dying swan.

Gurdjieff and his followers took for granted presumptions explored in the previous psychological and philosophical chapters: there is participation in reality in movement; and this participation is embodied – it is the movement of a whole person, not only activity of a knowing mind or of a physiological body, in structured relation with the world. The followers, and even Gurdjieff himself, though he 'inclined' to claim a special status, were 'of woman born', and the ritualistic use of movement built on the world of self and other in relations shaped from the earliest days of life. Leader and led found forms of relation in moving practices that, as they reported them, went deeper than other forms of cultural expression involving movement, like speaking or flower-arranging. For Gurdjieff and his followers, and for other like-minded people, moving relations existed between the person and the forces of nature, and thus, they believed, by cultivating appropriate exercises it was possible to restore the harmony of being in the world.

This and other examples show that many kinds of movement, though especially dance, make claims about access to some kind of reality. The appeal of modern dance appears to be the appeal of the real standing or even truth of the body, even though there is no agreement about what this reality really is. If so, perhaps it is possible after all to reach a general conclusion about dance. It is the conclusion explored in earlier chapters: the self and other are given in relations in movement, and dance is the aesthetics of these relations. (This, as discussed, leaves for debate the issue as to whether or not intuition of the self is original or derivative.)

There is more to say about dance culture after introducing walking. But before doing this it is pertinent to ask, not why people dance, but why people watch dance – and if we take TV and video into account, watch it in very large numbers. It is striking that audiences commonly sit still in order to watch movement. The question, why watch, leads into questions about the difference between live and recorded performance, a topical issue after the COVID pandemic and in the light of IT. Sport and teaching, as much as the arts, make it relevant to ask why people want to watch live performance. I suggest the key to an answer lies in this very language: actual physical presence is called '*live* performance'.

Live performance, like life itself is born and it dies: it passes and it is not repeated. Of course, dance has an after-life in memory and in recordings, and in this it is also like life. But the live performance is essentially ephemeral, and both performers and audiences know this, and in acting and watching they therefore engage with human finitude. There may be unparalleled intensity. It is not inappropriate to liken the performance to a rock-climb or to a walk on a tight-rope: the action risks a fall – death is not held at a distance but 'touched' (Lewis 2000). The imagination of engagement in a passing phenomenon, coloured by knowledge that there will be an end, intensifies the passions. By the time there is description, the event is already past. Moving and sensing movement mark the passage of time, and that marking is that much more explicit in the live performance.

Performers and audiences alike report the buzz that comes with successful collaboration – from the jam session where jazz musicians riff on each other's playing, to the spark both actors and audiences report with an especially successful piece of theatre, to the social rituals of the football match. Personal feelings interact with aesthetic traditions and social habits. A choreographer, interviewed during lockdown in the pandemic, highlighted the dimension perhaps most relevant to kinaesthesia: he longed, he said, to return to 'the sense of physicality' of live dance performance (Will Tuckett, in Dance Nation 2, 2020). Dancing people joined with friends to maintain their movement online during the pandemic; yet, they restored physically moving together in the same space as soon as possible with evident relief. Certainly, it is a matter of individual habit and social custom to get physically together, and going online both required and opened opportunities for new habits and customs. These new opportunities spectacularly include global reach and new aesthetic possibilities. In these ways, the pandemic speeded up social change that was, with new technologies, happening anyway. But is the change from offline to online performance in the arts simply a matter of change in habit and custom? The answer is surely, no. The old habits and customs have their reasons, as the previous discussion has explored in terms of the embodied character of the feel for reality given in kinaesthetic awareness. The choreographer who wanted to return to the 'physicality' of live performance expressed this reason.

The question why audiences appreciate dance has a large literature. One prominent approach argues that the observer of dance subjectively reproduces imagery or experiences elements of the movements and associated emotions perceived in the dancer. The American dance writer, John Martin, spread this understanding in the 1930s and 1940s, referring to 'kinesthetic sympathy' (Martin 1936, p. 114). Developing this argument, later writers have suggested that the viewer feels psychological *empathy*, more than sympathy, with the dancer, and shares elements of kinaesthetic experience (Sklar 1994, p. 14; Foster 2011; Reason and Reynolds 2010; Reynolds 2013; Lanzoni 2018). With the discovery of mirror neurons in the brain, the argument, seemingly backed by the neurosciences, gained new life. There is, however, wide individual variation in responsiveness, just as there is very wide individual variation in dance. The all-night witness of dance at a Hindu religious festival is not the same kind of observer as an enthusiast for the movements, originally selected by chance, in a performance choreographed by Merce Cunningham. Moreover, there may be a 'motor type' of individual especially sensitive to kinaesthetic awareness and, by contrast, there may be individuals who do not empathize at all with dancers. A leading example of the former was the friend of Vernon Lee (the pen name of Violet Paget, living in the decades on either side of 1900), the sculptor Clementina (Kit) Anstruther-Thomson. Lee and Anstruther-Thomson visited European galleries together, and Lee noted that her friend physically responded with movement and changes in breathing to art. These two women, I think, would have welcomed Emmanuel Levinas's summary:

> The world is not constituted as a static entity, directly delivered over to experience; it refers to 'points of view' freely adopted by a subject who, essentially, walks and possesses mobile organs ... Representation is directly relative to the subject's movements and to their positive possibility in kinaesthesis. (Levinas 1998, pp. 146–147)

Movement, and hence kinaesthetic feeling, makes a difference to the 'point of view' taken in relation to works of art and to the world at large. I too note how good it is to walk around sculptures and how intolerable it is for galleries to place sculptures in corners. There is also something to be said for walking towards and away from pictures as part of the act of looking. But I do not feel I empathize with dancers' movements. Rather, I feel I receive a gift: I am given something new, something which I did not previously have, and I feel that I share a world with the dancers. If people have a world in common, it does not need a special mind-brain function of empathy to achieve a relation between them, though empathy may of course (sometimes) be present.

It is plausible to think intimacy between people is possible because individual people, through their bodily senses and senses of movement, are intimate with themselves. The prototype for 'making contact' comes, to state the point once again, with the life-enacting process of action–resistance in movement. There is, therefore, an alternative to belief in a specific act of empathy at work in feeling close to others: there is a common, inter-subjective kinaesthetic constitution of the world. Humans share kinaesthetic worlds in common, and when a person moves, other people know something of the world as it is constituted for the moving person. 'It is a matter of taking part in a conjoint action through which there exists a unique world which is, at the same time, a world for several agents' (Berthoz and Petit 2008, p. 258, emphasis removed). When dancers move they create for the observers a world about which the observers already know a lot but do not know in the way the dancer has trained and been inspired to know. This enlarges the world for spectators. It is a gift (Foster 2019). And dancers enlarge a world of movement that audiences already know to some degree. Since a significant proportion of the audience for contemporary dance often consists of dancers, this pre-shared world is an important factor. The presence of the audience matters 'in turn' to the dancers as part of the resistance to their actions – resistances may be sweet as well as sharp – shaping movement. There are relations in both directions.

Dancers, whether participating in a religious ritual, performing in a black-box or letting go at a disco, have learned a social practice (even if they seek to change it), and so have the members of the audience (if there is one). Dancers and audiences share a social past in common, they share a body of customs and rules and they share expectations. They take for granted, and without reflection cannot escape, everything learned and felt in connection with movement from childhood and in everyday life. There is a very considerable kinaesthetic world in common behind every kind of performance. Avant-garde work seeks to go beyond this common world and break expectations, but it is still there. Indeed, the breaking of expectations occurs only because it is there. The choreographer who idealized the 'physicality' of live performance took for granted the habits and values at work in daily experience of physical contact.

Human relations are social achievements. It is possible to take any particular performance and ask what particular shared values the dance achieves (Foster 2019). Perhaps it is the beauty in the interaction of the dancers, perhaps it is dramatic spectacle (like a lift, for example), perhaps it is a political message (using movement, for instance, to repudiate gender distinctions), perhaps it is the wonder of youthful energy in full 'flow' and perhaps it is much else besides.

8   Walking

Dance slows into a walk (just as walking appears in contemporary dance performance). The feel of movement is not something unknown or esoteric but just there in everyday life, albeit customarily on the margins of awareness. Precisely this familiarity and taken-for-granted quality establishes a background for appreciating movement performances of all kinds. To explore this, I reflect on something many people like to do, walking. It is both a mundane activity (a person goes to the shop) and at times ecstatic (someone walks in the mountains). Comparable arguments, it should be clear, might be made about other forms of movement – cycling, aerobics, swimming, sports of all kinds – or alternative forms of movement, in wheelchairs, with prostheses or with white sticks.

It is a hugely emotional moment when a young child stands and staggers a few steps. No one will doubt the irreplaceable role of proprioception in this first 'step'. The learning thereafter is usually extremely rapid. Children move with high pleasure, which different social customs (like swaddling, play-pens, reins or simply being told not to fidget) markedly resist. In large parts of the world, children walk to school, and adults walk home from work. Rich people walk to raise money for charity, angry people walk to demonstrate against politicians, pilgrims walk ancient roads to holy sites and relatives and friends walk behind a coffin. All this walking, in some sense, involves felt movement.

Walking for pleasure, whether for long or short distances, is to a significant degree a modern phenomenon associated with the shift to urban life. Farmers who live all their lives in the countryside, if they have a choice, tend to opt for wheels on which to get around their land. Frédéric Gros's *Philosophy of Walking* described walking as the opportunity for city dwellers to return to themselves and away from the 'in one's face' life of the city and its commercial priorities. Walking

DOI: 10.4324/9781003368021-11

brings the possibility of presence, and for Gros presence is the antonym of commodity (Gros 2014). As he observed, the feeling of the steady, rhythmic movement of the walking body may substantially help a person return to quietness and to a feeling of the self undisturbed by other people and, particularly, institutions. The poet William Wordsworth, striding over the Lakeland Fells in north-west England, famously thought this. As Anne D. Wallace wrote, for Wordsworth, 'the natural, primitive quality of the physical act of walking restores the natural proportions of our perception, reconnecting us both with the physical world and with the moral order inherent in it' (Wallace 1993, p. 13). The practices which cultivate stillness and quiet self-centredness and specifically do not involve movement, like contemplation, nevertheless work in a comparable way, since these practices also involve intense proprioceptive activity. If walkers differ very considerably in their manner of walking – solitary or social, talking or quiet, thinking or unthinking – they nevertheless share movement in common, share a sense of movement in space and in time and a sense of the stable resistance of the ground. Walking, a person is 'grounded'. Discussing Henry David Thoreau, the author of *Walden*, Gros wrote:

> Walking is a matter not just of truth, but also of reality. To walk is to experience the real. Not reality as pure physical exteriority or as what might count as a subject, but reality as what holds good: the principle of solidity, of resistance. When you walk, you prove it with every step: the earth holds good. With every pace, the entire weight of my body finds support and rebounds, takes a spring. There is everywhere a solid base underfoot. (Gros 2014, p. 94)

Movement in space and time is movement in relation to a ground, action-resistance, and this ground is at one and the same time physical, moral and, for many people, spiritual. Movement is both unmediated expression and intimate metaphor of the human condition.

Walking is participation: a whole person, body and mind together, goes along a path, goes through a landscape or cityscape, or goes around a building.

Feet touch the ground, with the feel of bare feet or shod, and the ground bears a person's weight. A person might 'float along', or perhaps like a Victorian long-distance walker, 'pound along', and it might be 'easy going' or 'hard going'. The legs are light or heavy; the head is held up to look at the view or caste downwards to secure stability; arms swing or grasp sticks. Walkers know relations with what

Figure 8.1 Two men in a landscape. Photograph, Ruth O'Dowd. Courtesy of Ruth O'Dowd.

is around them because these relations change as they go along. Compare the walk with touring in a car or site-seeing in a new city from the top of a tourist bus. Motorized, the tourist gets an overview, sees a lot in a short time and, not least, is protected from the weather. But there is a glass wall between the tourist and the surroundings and the relationship is primarily visual. Walking people, by contrast, are 'in contact': they are active and the world around actively resists. Their feet are 'on the ground'; they participate in a more intimate way with the physical conditions – the weather, commonly enough, is an inescapable reminder of intimacy: the rain trickles down a neck, the hot sun burns a face. During a walk, a person stops to look at the view and, turning the body, 'takes in' a panorama, moving and feeling space and acquiring a perspective. Special and deep emotions 'surface' in outstanding landscapes or architecture, but also in deeply familiar but loved places, in settings which seem to force their nature into contact with a person and when all a person's senses seem to merge and there is something like presence. All this hinges on kinaesthesia and proprioception. It is just the same in everyday as in exotic movement: walking to the shop, there is a stupendous array of pavements, rails, walls, moving traffic, steps, architectural features to pass over or through or be in or step on. The quality of relations with the surroundings depends on movement, as architects and town planners appreciate and designers, even if they are concerned only with the movements of fingers, understand.

Relation to locality through landscape or cityscape is a marked feature of the poetic imagination: 'How precise the familiar hill paths remain for our muscular consciousness!' (Bachelard 1964, p. 11). No poet, to my knowledge, writes about the physiology of proprioception; but poets do write about the embodied feel of being in intimate relationship with a world, even when reason knows the physical world to be inanimate. This relationship builds on kinaesthesia. The Scottish poet Nan Shepherd spent a lifetime walking in the Cairngorms in all weather conditions and left a record of her love for this notoriously stony and harsh plateau in the Highlands (cold cloud may cover the mountains for a month at a time). She knew she related through her body and she ascribed knowledge to the body, and thereby she celebrated kinaesthetic knowledge. She wrote about how 'after hours of steady walking, with the long rhythm of motion sustained until motion is felt, not merely known by the brain, as the "still centre" of being'. And she continued: 'for as I penetrate more into the mountain's life, I penetrate more deeply into my own' (Shepherd 2011, pp. 106, 108; Andrews 2020). It is, Shepherd felt, not only movement of the whole body that matters; the power of vision itself depends on movement of the eyes. 'Moving the eye itself when looking at things that do not move, deepens one's sense of outer reality. Then static things may be caught in the very act of becoming' (Shepherd 2011, p. 10).

Not every walker has the quietness and patience of spirit for this kind of vision. But the growth in popularity in recent decades of urban as well as country walks, whether to appreciate history, ecology, architecture, literary associations or some other theme, suggests that there is public sympathy with these kinds of sensitivities. Many cities now have organized walking tours, themed to art or architecture, famous people or the environment, or to ghosts, building relations between people who stand and move but otherwise might not notice where and in relation to what. The artist Richard Long created ways both to record his walking in a landscape (for example, by arranging stones he found along the way) and to represent his walking in a gallery space (for example, by presenting maps marked to show how he had 'covered' a landscape). He observed: 'It's the touching and the meaning of the touching that matters' (reported by Ann Seymour, in Long 2002, p. 8). In the United Kingdom, there is a Walking-Artists Network focused on local spaces. Walking is one long tour around and through a piece of sculpture, the world. There is even 'the dance walk', a form of collective dancing 'in the street', in which dancers – and non-dancers too – display their relationship with the local, ordinary world around them. Moving in ways that make the public stare because they are so unusual and non-utilitarian, the dance asserts that the space belongs to people. The dance-walk reclaims the streets. I shared this with the Swiss performer, Foofwa d'imobilité, on the pavements and tarmac of Moscow. He has taken the idea around the world, dancing in utterly different places, making the local global.

Much has been made of Rousseau's walking, though walking was for him a means to think – 'my body must move if my mind is to do the same' (Rousseau 1996, p. 157) – not the means to experience movement. The walking mattered to Rousseau because it occasioned reverie, self-reflection. He wrote, influentially, of his belief that walking and reverie in solitude drew him close to his 'natural self', by which he meant the self who is not a self-conscious social actor. Rousseau claimed: 'These hours of solitude and meditation are the only time of the day when I am completely myself, without distraction or hindrance, and when I can truly say that I am what nature intended me to be' (Rousseau 2014, p. 11). This is the emblematic moment for walking understood as an aesthetic and political act of individual autonomy.

Figure 8.2 Dancewalk. Foofwa d'imobilité in Moscow, Russia, July 2017. Photograph, in the author's collection. By kind permission.

All the same, Rousseau did not deny himself contact with local people for talk or a glass of milk.

Turning to the hills and mountains, walkers in the nineteenth century, and in ever-increasing numbers thereafter, hiked from the industrial cities and bourgeois drawing-rooms 'back to nature'. The Edwardian walker A. H. Sidgwick pinpointed the local character of the sensibility conveyed through bodily knowledge in a walk:

> You cannot grasp the character of a country by a conscious effort of discursive reason; all you can do is set your body fairly to its task, and to leave the intimate character of your surroundings to penetrate slowly into your higher faculties, aided by the consciousness of physical effort, the subtle rhythm of your walk, the feel of the earth beneath your feet, and the thousand intangible influences of sense. (Sidgwick 1912, pp. 8–9)

Urban people turned to an accessible nature 'without', the landscape and its natural history, and by taking this step they turned to an accessible nature 'within', the living experience of being a person in motion in the world, being grounded ('standing on one's own two feet'). The argument deriving knowledge of reality from action-resistance was the philosophical partner of the walker in the hills and dales restoring the spirit of nature's reality and the spirit of human dignity. As was said of Wordsworth, 'liberty of mind accompanies liberty of movement, specifically the liberty of deliberate excursive walking' (Wallace 1993, p. 165).

Leslie Stephen, a veteran long-distance walker, emphatically belonged among those who, when they walked and climbed, did not consciously think and were silent. More precisely, Stephen understood that in walking a customary way of dividing reference to thinking and feeling broke down: in a walk, all his capacities became intimate with each other. Stephen described movement as the living expression of his personal integration, and it was beautiful.

> I do not speak merely of the physical state which supervenes upon a day of vigorous exercise in a pure atmosphere and amidst exquisite scenery; but rather of the sleep of the mind which may be enjoyed with open eyes and during the exertion of muscular activity ... But in my case, which I take to be an ordinary one, the brain active during walking (and the result is one of the great charms of that form of exercise) becomes merely an instrument for co-ordinating the muscular energies ... Thought, that is, becomes

indistinguishable from emotion. The outside world is not a collection of objects to be classified; it is merely the background of a dream; its presence is felt rather than perceived; it is like the tapestry of some gorgeous chamber which one vaguely watches with half-shut eyes during the initial stages of a quiet doze. (Stephen 1936, pp. 108–109)

This dream landscape, Stephen averred, is achieved when the body is active; the sense of movement is its necessary condition. His imagery of dozing, however, hardly did justice to other passages of his writing on climbing, appropriately often called 'scrambling', where he used the language of force, referring to both force 'within' and force 'without', the force of the body in contact with the resistant mountains. Straus, in his discussion of the significance of the human upright posture, also drew on figures of speech of rock and resistance.

Upright posture, which we learn in and through falling, remains threatened by falls throughout our lives. The actual stance of man is, therefore, 'resistance.' A rock reposes in its own weight. The things that surround us appear solid and safe in their quiet resting on the ground, but man's status demands endeavor. (Straus 1952, p. 536)

Stephen, Bruce Haley observed, walking and scrambling in the Alps, apprehended nature 'with his whole body. This measurement by muscular exertion, using healthy will and body together as means of cognition, gives one a sense of his own reality as well as that of his environment' (Haley 1978, p. 254). Haley went on to characterize Victorian mountain climbing as a matter of overcoming resistance, physical and mental, enabling climbers to find themselves. The climbers – and there were women too, in spite of the masculine tone of much Victorian writing on the subject – recreated in action the philosophical theory of knowledge that ascribed knowledge of reality to sensed movement-resistance.

For Stephen, 'the mountains represent the indomitable force of nature to which we are forced to adapt ourselves'. As a result, he asked: 'Where does Mont Blanc end, and where do I begin?' (Stephen 1936, pp. 180–181). Climbing enacted in individual lives the correlation of the forces of nature and the forces of human activity which scientists were discussing as the latest insight, the physics of the conservation of energy. Force was known in felt movement and kinaesthetic sense.

A striking number of people who write abstract theory have also been walkers or climbers. From the way he talked about rock, I surmise that Merleau-Ponty was a climber (Morrison 2009). When he wrote about embodied perception, he knew what he was talking about from climbing as a young man:

> Our body, to the extent that it moves itself about, that is, to the extent that it is inseparable from a view of the world and is that view itself brought into existence, is the condition of possibility ... of all expressive operations and all acquired views which constitute the cultural world. (Merleau-Ponty 2002, p. 451)

He also wrote: 'my existence as subjectivity is merely one with my existence as a body and with the existence of the world' (Merleau-Ponty 2002, p. 475). These are words, one may imagine, a climber would use, *were the climber reflecting rather than doing*. 'Finding a foothold' and 'losing one's footing', acquiring and losing a place in the world, are the figures of speech of the climb. Rock-climbers record a special interest in 'how the rock feels' to the senses of touch and movement (Dutkiewicz 2015, p. 29).

The appreciation of movement in a landscape or cityscape – 'the concern for the kinesthetics of landscape experience' – has significant resonance with environmental awareness (Veder 2013, p. 6). The walker is in a position to have knowledge of surroundings because of 'moving' participation in them, in a way a person 'just looking' is not. A person has a different relationship with a landscape, a sculpture or a building when moving in or around it, as opposed to having the stance of a passive observer. The active and passive relationship differ in ways which are cognitive, emotional, ethical and political, as well as kinaesthetic.

Viewed in wider social perspective, walking and climbing, in this like sport and the performing arts, find a voice for asserting and critiquing relations between 'natural' individual bodies and 'nature', escaping from, or transcending, social conditions which people judge to be 'non-natural'. The creators of modern dance made much of rejecting balletic movement for natural movement, though this did not stop them thinking that the achievement of natural movement required long training. As this suggests, all references to 'nature' and 'natural' are evaluative and relative to the particulars of social context. In modern times, for instance, the ground on which people stand has literally changed, with asphalt and escalators, while softly shod feet have certainly changed its feel. But before discussing the social agency and resistance in movement, there is more to say on the movement of dance.

Nietzsche was another walker, in the mountains and valley of the Engadin in Switzerland, and he walked, like Rousseau, to encounter himself and to think. And dance, as all Nietzsche's readers have observed, was for him a key figure of speech.

9 The dance of life

Nietzsche is indelibly associated with the figure of his imagination, the god-like human, Zarathustra, about whom the author said, 'does he not go along like a dancer?' (Nietzsche 1969a, p. 40). The central feature of Nietzsche's figures of speech encompassing dance is the representation of dance as life, a picture of exuberant individual movement of body and thought, which Nietzsche drew to make a contrast with the congealed movements and ideas demanded by social conformity and philosophical convention. Dance, Nietzsche held, distinguishes the strong individual, the person able to stand apart and to voice the reality of 'the will to power': 'Lift up your hearts, my brothers, high, higher! And do not forget your legs! Lift up your legs, too, you fine dancers; and better still, stand on your heads!' (Nietzsche 1969a, pp. 304–305).

The interpretation of Nietzsche's writings is itself a huge enterprise. But perhaps enough has been said to signal why language about movement in the form of dance captured his readers' imagination. His language about individual action-resistance pictured the power which would, readers felt, enable superior people to live better than bourgeois or proletarian worlds permitted. He had many readers, like Duncan, who were, or who wished to be, artists, and these artists brought about the modernist turn at the beginning of the twentieth century. While 'modernism' subsumes many forms, across the whole range the artist asserted the right and power to create and judge art authentic to life. This upset traditions of aesthetic judgment. The sensibility Nietzsche fostered, though naturally the outward forms have changed, has never really gone from the world of modern dance. Whatever the contradictions of modern times, the act of dancing, like the act of juggling, may hope to keep things 'in the air' and prevent things 'sinking into the mire'. This is 'life'. Dancers and choreographers have continued to assert the ways this is to be achieved. They are

DOI: 10.4324/9781003368021-12

Figure 9.1 A frieze copied from Ancient Greece depicting dancing figures of men and women. Process print, 1921. Wellcome Collection. Public domain mark.

tacitly committed to another Nietzschean dictum: 'Dancing is not the same thing as staggering wearily back and forth between different impulses. High culture will resemble a daring dance, thus requiring ... much strength and flexibility' (Nietzsche 2004, p. 169).

During and after Nietzsche's lifetime (he died in 1900), there was considerable enthusiasm for philosophies of life, worldviews finding a guiding force attributable to life itself at work in evolutionary and historical progress. For many, like the playwright George Bernard Shaw, life-force was the human expression of cosmic forces or powers. Theosophists, influenced by Madame Blavatsky, melded belief in these powers with esoteric traditions drawn from India. Rudolf Steiner recast the beliefs as anthroposophy, and he sought to create organic harmonies in architecture (pioneering organic form in concrete in the Goetheanum at Dornach, near Basel) and in dance movements in which his followers move in tune with hidden powers. In the studio of musical movement, 'Heptachor', which Rudneva helped found in Saint-Petersburg in 1913, seven young women collectively sought to practise movements in tune with breathing, responding to the harmony, melody and rhythm of classical music played on the piano. In the utopian commune which existed at Monte Verità in the Swiss Ticino, Rudolf Laban, in the years just before World War I, organized free dance, free to the extent of dancing naked in nature. In his own studio teaching, then and later, he envisaged postures which demonstrated the common geometric structure between the macrocosm, the world, and the microcosm, the human person. Moving among the artistic avant-garde, he made a large claim for the centrality of movement to the modernist innovations then underway: 'We dancers are the pioneers of the new dawn of art' (quoted in Sirotkina 2021, unpaginated). Laban knew and at times worked with figures like Wigman, Kurt Jooss and Hilde Holger who were central to European dance in the twentieth century, as well as Josef Pilates, a pioneer of movement as therapy.

Graham self-consciously built her technique on breathing, understood as 'the pulsation of life':

> Every time you breathe life in or expel it, it is a release or a contraction. ... You are born with the two movements and you keep both until you die. But you begin to use them consciously so that they are beneficial to the dance dramatically. You must animate that energy within yourself. Energy is the thing that sustains the world and the universe. It animates the world and everything in it. (Graham 1992, p. 46)

It is hard to imagine a more direct affirmation of dance as the dance of life.

Laban, for his part, is remembered for having devised a system of movement analysis and dance notation, choreology. This work reflected the way he viewed forms of human movement as the expression or symbolism of real, natural forces. It followed that it should be possible to establish a science of movement forms. Creating such a science, the first step was objective and precise description of different dance movements. This in its turn required notation, a language, equivalent to musical notation, to represent an art form not originally existing as a language. Laban's notation system, first elaborated in the 1920s, had influence in later performance theory and continues to be taught. He 'analysed what he called the "effort" qualities of movement in terms of degrees of resistance to weight, space, time and flow' (Reynolds 2013, p. 220), implicitly referring to kinaesthetic sensibility. He was not alone in these efforts. In Moscow, also in the 1920s, the new Bolshevik state funded an institution intended to be a scientific academy for the arts as a whole, the State Academy of Artistic Sciences (GAKhN). Following up the inspirational example of Vassily Kandinsky, who believed that there are underlying principles in symbolism linking colour, form, sound and movement, the academy undertook experimental work with dancers. It also had a laboratory specifically for choreology, founded by Aleksei Sidorov.

> Sidorov was interested in dance primarily as an observer, photographer and art scholar; he wanted to stand firmly on the ground of

empirical science and, for this sake, he analyzed and classified various movements, examined the visual image the body of the dancer produces against various backgrounds, in different costumes or indeed naked. In the Choreolab, his assistants compared types of gait, in shoes, on high heels or barefoot, in skirt, in tunic, of a nude person ... What they were looking for was a *picture* which the dancer, choreographer and stage designer create together for the enjoyment of the observer. Sidorov believed that dance is in the eye of the beholder; in his choreology there is much more of the objectifying *gaze* of a photographer or an iconographer. (Sirotkina 2021, unpaginated)

Following these lines, Sidorov worked more in the style of the descriptive analysis of painting established by the Swiss-German art scholar, Heinrich Wölfflin, than in the style of the avant-garde theoretician, Laban, who developed analysis out of his own practice. Both Sidorov and Laban, however, shaped their thinking in the light of esoteric traditions and practices, seeing in aesthetic movement relations with the hidden structure of the world. Laban referred to 'the sacred geometry of space' (quoted in Sirotkina 2021, unpaginated). With the cultural and political 'break' in Russia in 1929 to 1932, the work of the Moscow experimental laboratory was brought to a halt. Soviet power re-established the position of classical ballet, while also creating a new, social realist form of folk-dance. Laban attempted briefly in the 1930s to put his ideals to work in the service of the Nazi state, but this failed and he moved to England.

Interestingly, Gibson, the psychologist of perception, drew in a reference to (Laban's) dance notation (Gibson 1966, p. 121). Gibson was concerned to delineate the facts of haptic perception, especially the capacity to discriminate very small degrees of movement or angular positioning in joints. As he pointed out, as early as the 1880s Alfred Goldscheider, manipulating the passive fingers on a subject's hand, had shown just how refined this discrimination of movement could be. Gibson looked for ways to describe felt movement, and in the process he noted the daunting complexity this description would have to assimilate, not least because there are about one hundred movable joints in the skeletal body. Attempts to create dance notation have also had to struggle with this refinement and complexity of movement, which presupposes the refinement and complexity of the kinaesthetic-proprioceptive system.

It was a short step from the ideals of early free dance to modern forms of movement therapy. If belief that cosmic powers inform progress in human lives did not, for many people, survive the horrors of European events, the practices that had formerly been associated with those powers and appeared usable in the pursuit of individual health certainly did. Dance therapy, Pilates, Alexander Technique and many forms of physiotherapy have flourished in the past century or so, effecting constructive compromise between ideals of human flourishing, medical views of health, organizational goals of efficiency and financial interests in having a return on investment in educational training. In this context, the language of movement and action, once again presupposing kinaesthetic sensibility, has proved apt for the description of individual human goals of good living (or 'wellness'), more apt indeed than languages describing only mental life or only brain processes.

Therapists have drawn on both physiological and phenomenological traditions of research, and a combination of these traditions and therapeutic goals informs theories of embodied cognition, as discussed earlier. Fuchs, to take an eminent instance, has stressed the emotional content of bodily well-being in studies focused on proprioception and the conjoined material and psychological meanings of 'moving' and 'being moved' in depressive and autistic conditions (Fuchs and Koch 2014). Meaning and emotional satisfaction emerge, it is said, in lives of movement, when body, mind and place in a social group work together and create coordinated meaning:

> It is embodied subjects who coordinate, which means that in these couplings there is also a coordination of *meaning*. In fact, meanings emerge, become aligned, change and so on through the interpersonal coordination of movements. And vice versa, movements also become coordinated through attempts at understanding each other, which is an effort to create or align understandings. (Fuchs and De Jaegher 2009, p. 471)

Dancers create interpersonal meaning at the level of shared movements presented as performance, and the emotional content of this is very important to performers and audiences alike. Linguistic roots indicate as much: 'to emote' is to bring forth affective content. The ancient history of the conception of passion concerned its nature as 'suffering' (as opposed to acting), that is, a state of being moved by something. The language still refers to 'a moving performance'. Hence, in dance therapy, widely practised with people who may not be responsive to verbal therapies, such as autistic children or elderly people with dementia, movement is used to create emotional relations.

Proprioceptive and kinaesthetic capacities persist when cognitive ones may be limited.

Dance, however, is fabulously varied, and it would be wrong to view all dance movement as concerned with establishing meaning in relations. There is also an interest in innovative movement for its own sake, and, indeed, in detaching movement from accepted canons of meaning. Cunningham's choreographic work, for instance, sought forms of movement not found in nature: at one stage, he required dancers to achieve movements selected by chance procedures and for which they had not been trained.

Owing to the scientific and medical interest in motor control, bodily habits and acquired skills, and also because of sports science, a large literature has consolidated around what the psychologist Howard Gardner called 'bodily-kinesthetic intelligence' (Gardner 1993, pp. 206–237). It is everyday knowledge that in accomplishing a movement task, like hitting a target, the non-conscious body 'knows' what to do and that some people have a special aptitude for such tasks. References to bodily intelligence stress that the body does indeed have a kind of knowing, or 'knowing without thinking' as Zdravko Radman called it, though perhaps carried through by the same nervous processes as those underlying conscious action (Radman 2012). In the background is common sense appreciation that much everyday action, as well as specialist skill in movement, depends on tacit knowledge, knowledge 'known to the body' but not consciously articulated 'in the mind'. Ordinary language refers with decisive insight to 'hands-on knowledge', knowledge gained through embodied interaction with the world. In the light of such thinking, Yvonne Rainer, in 1966, created one of the most influential pieces of contemporary dance under the title, 'The mind is a muscle. Part I (Trio A)'.

Before Gardner, the social scientist Marcel Mauss, in a deceptively simple lecture on 'Body techniques' in 1934, introduced the term *habitus* to describe embodied habits of movement skill (Mauss 1979). He discussed movement in a context where he was concerned with integrating the biological, the psychological *and the social* conditions which shape movement, and his proposals underlay a great deal of subsequent inquiry into movement culture in the arts.

If the body has its own intelligence, this seems to vindicate a search, in dance or in other forms of movement, for 'natural' as opposed to 'artificial' technique: to move naturally is to let the body organize movement for itself; to move artificially is to move with socially acquired habits. Some dancers (like those in the Duncan tradition) have confessed to spending many years *learning* to move *naturally*.

This sounds odd. But there is no paradox in learning to move naturally if it is thought that society has trained a person as a child to learn artificial forms of movement, movements guided by social reason and not by innate proprioceptive patterns. Iris Marion Young's much cited study of 'Throwing like a girl' discussed the manner in which girls as opposed to boys learn to throw or run awkwardly (Young 1980). As such studies show, a lot of prejudgment goes into statements about what is natural, and a good deal of movement thought to be natural may be learned. As the flourishing in recent decades of women's sports previously restricted to men, such as football (soccer) and boxing, has shown, differences in performance have been at least very substantially acquired. All this is of close interest to the dancer.

It is also of obvious importance to sports psychology, and because of the competitive and financial interests at stake there is a lot of discussion. It has long been well recognized that imagery, that is, the plan or schema – however this psychological content is formulated – plays a significant part in preparation for performance. Psychologists and physiologists have therefore taken a keen interest in kinaesthetic images and the anticipation of performance in training. There are different theories of what is involved; for instance, sports psychologists defending the widely held 'neuromuscular theory' argue that athletes, picturing an action in anticipation, put into use the neurons that will actually be involved in achieving the action. It is also widely held that athletes train and then do not think about action when the competitive moment comes; instead, they concentrate on motivation, the passion to win. Many sports trainers maintain that conscious thinking about carrying out a movement, such as launching oneself into a sprint, distracts from rather than enhances achievement. This may not be correct (Montero 2016; Gallagher 2018). There is at least reason to be uneasy at analyses in terms that separate the intelligent body and the emotional or motivated mind, not least because bodily actions appear to deploy reasoning, while emotional and motivational states may be non-conscious. The approach of embodied cognition here proves its worth, as it makes it possible to talk intelligibly about the achievement of tasks across the conscious/non-conscious border.

The analysis of dance, following Mauss, involves understanding movement as at one and the same time a bodily process (involving proprioception and motor control), a psychological event (involving kinaesthesia and affect), and a social action (involving gesture and aesthetic performance). An individual embodied habitus grows from bodily techniques of motility learned in interaction with teachers and other dancers, that is, through dancers training to move individually (but still socially) in particular ways, in particular spaces and over particular spans of time.

Dancers acquire a tacit understanding of skills necessary to fulfil the judgment, 'I can'. This, however, is also a judgment, 'we can', as they do not generally perform alone. This inherence of the social world in dance is also central to dance as therapy. Some dance groups, indeed, project collective learning in movement as the basis for moral and political cooperative living, even for the regeneration of community, building on the inescapable reality that to move is to be in relations and hence in emotional 'contact' (Foster 2011).

There are forms of dance that explicitly explore relations by recreating them in 'artificial' ways which open new possibilities. 'Site-specific' movement is dance (whether choreographed or improvised) responsive to the particular space and architecture of a landscape or building; it creates a form of moving sculpture. The dance-walk is an expansive version of this form. Bodily movements in such dance exhibit a particularly rich appreciation of the active nature of perception,

Figure 9.2 Musical movement. Studio 'Terpsihora', Moscow, Russia, December 2019. Photograph, Alexei Sedov. In the author's collection.

and dance thereby becomes a living study in embodied cognition. From the early 1970s, following Steve Paxton's experimental work in New York, there has been a large dance interest in the particularities of physical relations between people in actual contact, not only of the relations of people in space and time. The resulting techniques of 'contact improvisation' developed learning to touch, take the weight, feel the balance, trust the hold and mediate the fall between dance partners. It is self-evident that this exploration of physical relations has psychological, moral and social content (Brandstetter 2013). In particular, it has proved to be a form of dance open to explorations of the meaning and power relations of gender.

The action of moving together with other people, whether in dance or as part of a sports team or in a military parade or in an orchestra, has a deeply significant place in feelings of identity. This is also true for participation in political 'movements'. To develop perspectives on this, it is necessary to discuss more closely the social nature of movement by considering movement as gesture and as agency.

Part IV
Fourth movement: allegro

10 Gesture

Feeling one's body, feeling movement and feeling touch are personal, individual and in many circumstances intimate and private dimensions of life. Each element of awareness of movement brings a wondrous quality to the subjective sense of being human. In Levinas's words: 'The corporeal gesture is not a nervous discharge but a celebration of the world, a poetry. The body is a feeling felt' (Levinas 1966, p. 40). However individual, though, these feelings are also social; they have both a subjective feel and objective relations to objects, events and people. 'Relations are inseparable from affective tone, or concern. And affective tone is inseparable from the modes that relations create and through which relations move. The becoming-body of dance is the composition of a relation' (E. Manning 2009, p. 40). Even when no one else is there and you move by yourself, being there in a particular space and time has content for you through what you have previously learned as social activity. Every movement that a person makes (and the 'movement' may be the maintenance of stillness) is a potential communication as well as a rearrangement of physical coordinates. Each movement and each posture is a potential gesture. Whether it is perceived as a gesture depends on whether the moving person knows and follows a social code, and on whether an observer receives the movement as communication. The movement does not have to be conscious or planned. Presumably, the child in the womb does not plan to kick, though the mother may well feel the child communicates. In addition, humans certainly understand much animal movement as communication and, through gesture, animals and humans use movement to build up relations. Further, without presupposing anything about the origins and development of language, it is clear that what is the case for gesture is the case for speech and writing in all their forms. The proprioceptive system, which underlies all movement achieving gesture, underlies social life.

DOI: 10.4324/9781003368021-14

At times, psychologists have treated visible and recordable movement, including speech movements, as the key to making psychology an objective science, eliminating reference to subjective mental states. Scientists, the argument goes, cannot observe the mental states of other people, but they can observe what people do. Hence, it has been argued that psychology must develop as the science of doing, that is, of *behaviour*. This way of thinking persists among contemporary neuroscientists, a number of whom assert that observing what people do and correlating this with what their neurons do is the only way to make an objective human science. The scientists and philosophers combining the approaches of embodied cognition and phenomenology, though they also research activity rather than mental states, reject this and include the purposes, symbolism and semantics of gesture and speech as the proper subject matter of human science. This inclusion is essential for the perspectives offered here and for addressing human-centred questions, like why people dance.

Kinaesthesia and gesture, the inner and the outer faces of movement, together form a world of meaning. As Levinas wrote:

> We are not the subject of the world and a part of the world from two different points of view; in expression we are subject and part at once ... We know through gesture how to imitate the visible and to coincide *kinesthetically* with the gesture *seen*: in perception our body is also the 'delegate of *Being*'. (Levinas 1966, p. 41)

There is a world of shared meaning because of the inherent commonality of inner feeling and outer, visible gesture. Posture, which is kinaesthetically informed gesture, illustrates this. Sander L. Gilman built his historical study of posture on this understanding: 'Posture is simultaneously of the mind and the body ... The way our body imagines itself in the world is the product of our sense of posture and of the cultural meanings attached to that sense' (Gilman 2018, pp. 18–19). In the mid-nineteenth century, François Delsarte, in the interest of coaching singers, orators and actors, pioneered the systematic examination of the voice, breathing and movement in order to list and classify the emotional meaning of posture and gesture. This work entered the physical culture world and modern dance performances in the early twentieth century. The gracious movement of the carved relief of Gradiva, discussed by Freud, revealed in her gait the walk of a goddess. As Andreas Mayer also noted, Balzac believed the gait of a woman revealed her intentions (Mayer 2012).

Children from an early age know how to 'read' gestures since, except in conditions of extreme deprivation, from birth a person is in continuous interpersonal relations mediated by gestural dialogue. (Knowledge of gestural movements has been called *kinesis*.) 'Reading' gesture is possible because people share a background in common, that is, they share a world giving rise to shared sense of movement. Guillemette Bolens illustrated the argument by placing at the front of her book on gesture a coloured plate of the beautiful painting by J.-B.-S. Chardin, created in 1737–1738, of a boy who watches attentively the small wooden top he has set spinning. Looking at the painting, the viewer 'sees' the boy's sense of movement. He himself is standing still, but his pose gestures and refers the viewer not so much to what is 'in his mind' but to a social space, an experience in common, the viewer shares with the boy. As Bolens commented: 'The comprehension of tropes relies heavily on the reader's ability to perceptually simulate and dynamically situate conceptual constructs' (Bolens 2012, p. 16; also Josipovici 1996, chapter 23). Gesturing is not only a matter of utilizing a common vocabulary of movements but of creating new possibilities in relations: 'the body must be seen as a series of processes of becoming, rather than as a fixed state of being' (Elizabeth Grosz, quoted in Bolens 2012, p. 51). Implications for dance follow: the dancing body, whatever else it may do, gestures, and much of the interest and aesthetics of contemporary dance comes with pursuing new gestures, new forms of 'becoming', which dancer and audience share, just as they share kinaesthetic awareness. So well is this appreciated that some choreographers have set out to subvert the world of shared and accepted gestures by devising forms of movement due to chance, to properties of the physiological body or to some other factor that may be thought to escape the world of semantic reference. It remains the case, though, that 'reading' the motion of dancing bodies has been the focus of much academic dance study. Jane Desmond summarized the interest as a series of questions:

What is kinaesthetic subjectivity? How does it shape and get shaped by other social formations of the self, and of communities? How and what do we come to know through kinesthesis as a historically particular register of meaning? How do we theorize it? How does it relate to visual perception and systems of visual representation? (Desmond 1997, p. 2)

Such questions ensure that even when choreographers or dancers intend non-gestural movement, the performance of the movement embodies this intention as a gestural statement comprehensible in a particular artistic world. At the cutting edge of contemporary dance, performers often perform before an audience largely made up of people who themselves dance and who, consequently, have much experience with a common world, or community, of subjective kinaesthetic feeling and objective gesture.

Awareness of embodiment, informed kinaesthetically, is central to a person's pre-reflective experience of things making sense and to the notion that this sense-making occurs for a self. The process of sense-making, conjoining kinaesthetic sensibility and gesture proceeds throughout life, establishing the basis for viable human relations: 'In fact, meanings emerge, become aligned, change and so on through the interpersonal coordination of movements. And vice versa, movements also become coordinated through attempts at understanding each other, which is an effort to create and align understandings' (Fuchs and De Jaegher 2009, p. 471). Psychologists working in the phenomenological tradition have explored this aligning of human activity, contributing to medical and ethnological studies of the social worlds made possible by gesture. For example, F. J. J. Buytendijk, working in the Netherlands in the mid-twentieth century, directed research on the creation of meaning through the interaction of moving people, such as people shaking hands or playing tennis, as well as publishing a general theory of posture and movement.

Reference to meaning-making by a self, through socially embedded movements, raises difficulties. It is somewhat notorious that different notions of the self are at work in contemporary discussions and that there is marked disagreement in references to the self. Historically, felt action, movement and resistance have had a large place in formulations of the notion of the human self, and mention has been made earlier of claims that awareness of action-resistance is the source of the very division of reality into self and other. French writers around 1800, discussing the origins of the notion of people as selves, concluded that belief in the self, and hence grammatical reference to the first-person 'I', is a deduction from living through action-resistance. This was a very intellectualist or cognitive understanding, and Maine de Biran went beyond it to intuit a more romantic and Catholic view of the self as a pre-existing reality known directly in willed action. Modern discussions re-open debate about whether the notion of self derives from elemental sensory phenomena or whether there is a pre-reflective notion of self given in being conscious. Numerous contemporary neuroscientists and scholars in the humanities, if for different reasons, tend to deny that there are irreducible selves; the notion of the self, they say, is acquired. The argument is that the self is a moral and a social construct: there has to be a certain kind of moral tradition and social organization for selves (as opposed to biological human organisms) to exist. By contrast, ordinary speech and 'folk psychology' (to use the American-English term for everyday psychological reasoning) commonly talks about the self as given and even searches for 'the true self'. Some psychologist-philosophers support a refined version of this view: Gallagher and Zahavi, after laying out the issues, concluded that people do have a first-order awareness of ownership and agency, that is, that there is a given 'I' in elemental form in conscious being (Gallagher and Zahavi 2021, chapter 10). Phenomenological approaches in psychology, indeed, tend to conclude that a pre-reflective intuition of self, to which embodied proprioception decisively contributes, is necessary for reflective awareness. This is persuasive argument. Accepting its validity, however, still leaves it open to argue for the constructed nature, by some combination of biological and social factors, of the particular character of each self.

As the gestural self merges into the speaking self, it appears natural to theorize about the evolutionary origins of language in the guttural and exclamatory noises accompanying early human movements. Modern sound poetry, in turn, enunciates sound elements, or phonemes, for their sensory rather than their semantic content. Vincent Barras, for example, has composed long pieces of articulated sound systematically working through the patterns of sounds in very different languages. Performing the sounds requires significant effort, muscular control, regulation of breathing and sensibility to what the tongue and throat are doing, confirming the importance of proprioception. It is also quite common for contemporary dance performers to use sound, from heavy breathing to cries of pain and laughter to speeches, enacting the continuity of words and movement. Sometimes the sound becomes a form of reflection on what the dancer is doing while exploring movement.

Generally speaking, until recently writers on the history of the arts did not give much attention to subjectively felt movement in the human body. This has changed. Reynolds drew attention to the importance of movement for the modernist arts in her studies of symbolist aesthetics in poets like Mallarmé and painters like Kandinsky, and also in her studies of energy in dance (Reynolds 1995; 2007). Veder and Brain discussed the importance of kinaesthesia, or proprioception, to the modernist arts early in the twentieth century (Brain 2015; Veder 2015). Zeynep Çelik Alexander extended the discussion to the world of design, though she enlarged the notion of kinaesthesia to encompass all forms of bodily, intuitive and tacit knowing, rather than focusing on a more specific sense of movement (Alexander 2017). Irina Sirotkina and I wrote on the importance of the sense of movement to poets and artists as well as dancers in revolutionary Russia (Sirotkina and Smith 2017).

Bringing together studies of gesture has opened possibilities for a general, or theoretically elaborated, account of performance in all its variety. Richard Schechner, writing and teaching accessible and very wide-ranging books and classes, shaped a field, performance studies, for this. (He first published *Performance Theory* in 1977.) He drew on ethnology, on observations of performance practices around the world, embedding Western knowledge of gesture and speech in an understanding applicable to rituals and traditions more widely (Schechner 2003). By this route, disciplined studies of embodied movement in gesture, dance and ritual have become an important medium for cultural comparison and interchange, and for the egalitarian ideals that have gone with multicultural projects. Very many performers in the arts, who naturally all move in one way or another, have come to see and appreciate both objective movement and the subjective feel of movement as social and political engagement.

Movements do not last: they take place and then they are gone. But, of course, just as the movements producing speech before aural recording were turned into material memory in the form of writing and books, so photography, film and video now turn movement into recorded performance. Performance theory has therefore taken on board not just movement but the media that preserve the movement and transmit it to new audiences. Media, however, mediate, that is, affect, shape and change the original. The assessment of this requires inquiry into who or what does what to whom, and for this we need an understanding of agency. Indeed, the issue of the relation between agency and felt movement has been in the background throughout the previous chapters.

11 Agency

To describe someone, or some condition or event, as alive, and even more to describe something as lively, is to attribute activity. To attribute *agency* is to go further and to identify and name the source of the movement and activity, whether individual or collective, as human. Agency is an attribute assigned to a person (or to a group or to an institution for this purpose considered as comparable to a person) when, in a socially agreed judgment, the person (or group or institution) is held to be the significant cause of something. It matters a great deal socially and legally that the attribution assigns intention and responsibility.

Agency is absolutely central to what there is to say about the feel of movement. Belief in individual agency, grounded in phenomenal awareness of the self as an effective force in movement, is pivotal to contemporary cultural references to kinaesthesia. I have discussed dance as the model instance of living movement, but the same issues feature in connection with sports and, indeed, in connection with all the small movements of everyday life (as comments on walking illustrated). The issues are of inestimable importance in politics. In stripped-down form the argument is this: people who feel they have little control over larger dimensions of the world in which they live turn to the body, to their own bodies and the movements they can accomplish, as the source and expression of agency. They also turn to the clothing and presentation of their bodies. Feeling movement is emblematic of self-attributed agency: 'It is ultimately kinesthetic experience, the somatic attention accorded to the lived sensation of movement, that allows the subject to become an agent in the making of herself' (Noland 2009, p. 171). Dance relates people to interpretations of who they are and to their surroundings: 'through kinaesthesia and empathy, the political citizen comprehends both the internal and external constructions of their personal social condition' (Steinman 2011,

DOI: 10.4324/9781003368021-15

pp. 59–60). People may even trust that in moving their own bodies they effect movement on the wider social stage: as a movement artist averred, 'we *are* the revolution' (Lannen 2020, p. 41). The political demonstration is the collective embodiment of this belief, however much participants may be well aware of making symbolic statements, making gestures, rather than having a literal effect. The body as a source of aesthetic knowledge has been linked to the aspiration that collective movement of bodies in political actions will lead to larger change: 'what moves as a body, returns as the movement of thought' (E. Manning 2009, p. ix).

The term agency characterizes the social state in which people judge that either other people or they themselves, as individuals or as members of a group, have power to effect change in the world around them. The judgment may be realistic or it may not. It may be noted that attribution of agency, in this usage, reaches no conclusion about freedom of the will. Whether people are really free is a philosophical question, and it is sufficient for present perspectives to distinguish, as a social matter, between free subjects, subjects with the power to do what they themselves decide to do, and people who are in this respect unfree objects, people whose activity results from forces beyond their control. In everyday life there is constant negotiation of attribution of agency to self and to other people, institutions and forces of nature (in this context, significantly including a person's own body). These attributions are culturally relative, complex and, often enough, contradictory. As Claid, writing as a dancer and a therapist interested in deliberate 'falling', observed: 'Falling, we are powerless subjects *and* agents of change. This paradoxical tension remains ever present' (Claid 2021, p. 2).

Reference to agency is often not clear-cut. This is partly due to an older usage of words, in which reference to an agent denotes any kind of thing (or person or institution) with the power to cause an effect, like a chemical 're-agent' in a manufacturing process. Twentieth-century literature in the philosophy of mind and social science, however, assigned special status to the word agency when used to describe attributed *human* capacity to act in the light of human purposes. This consolidated a highly positive view of agency as a social ideal. The older reference to agents as objects, though, persisted alongside this usage. More recently, certain social scientists have advocated treating on a level in explanatory terms all the causal factors involved in events, non-human factors as well as human factors. Adopting this practice, a social scientist analysing a car accident, for example, describes a brake mechanism and a human lack of concentration in the same terms as far as causal agency is concerned. There is reference to 'actor networks' and to explanation of events by reference to the interaction of the different factors (the 'actors') which are agents in bringing about the event, regardless of whether these factors, in everyday language, are human or non-human (Law and Hassard 1999). This might be attractive descriptive language for writers on embodiment as it breaks away from the evaluative hierarchies embedded in language about agency, language which separates higher and lower, human and animal and mind and body. It also resonates with contemporary rejection of humanism, that is, rejection of emphasis on the human as a distinct and unique ideal. Radical forms of art and movement have indeed attributed agency to flesh, body fluids, drugs, un-aesthetic clothing and violent bodies, and in this way they have explored and exposed conventional views about what can and cannot be done in movement. For example, Martin O'Brien, a person with cystic fibrosis, a genetic condition that cannot be cured, has used performance to give agency to all the dimensions of himself. He created social spaces, like lying in a coffin and coughing 'from beyond the grave', in which his physical condition obtains a social force, or agency, which it otherwise does not have.

In the contemporary Western world, dancers very commonly report experience of dance as experience of agency. There is reason, looking back on Duncan and other pioneers of modern dance, to refer to *free* dance. In dance, as in sport, performers show what the individual body can do if a person chooses. Dancing individually or collectively, or performing sports, individuals demonstrate, gesture, share identity and assert agency and power. Agency in movement is bound up with cutting-edge inquiry into self-identity and into 'the standing' of different self-identities in the polity. As a result, movement performance has been a hugely significant medium for the exploration of different views about ethnicity and gender. Movement practices foster self-respect and individual freedoms, and through collective practice they create a shared voice and, as it may be, an enlarged sense of agency. Whether or not the dancer, while moving, pays attention to the feeling of movement, the dancer demonstrates power and agency, thereby showing tacit appreciation of kinaesthetic awareness.

Agency is a central concept in performance and dance studies, linking discussion of the psychology and physiology of movement to discussion of political and ethical life. The incisive work of Carrie Noland well illustrates this. Noland's claim, and hope, was that self-aware movement opens a zone of individual freedom in a world of socially constituted and disciplined bodies. To make this claim plausible, she first engaged with a long-standing and ongoing debate in feminist studies (but not only feminist studies). The question at issue is whether accounts which focus on the embodied nature of being a woman (or a person) render women (or people) as material things with no special agency. Such accounts, perhaps bolstered by appeals to the neurosciences, would seem to conclude that the gendered body and its habits and customs necessarily derive from objective conditions, whether in biology or society. Such accounts therefore make it appear wrong to attribute agency, in a positively evaluative way, to women (or people). Noland, however, argued that the unpredictable variety and range of individual differences of kinaesthetic experience accompanying movement, and the boundless scope of gesture or visible movement, does in fact create social space for the kind of personal agency called freedom. Training, dancers (like other specialists in bodily movement) most certainly inscribe patterns of movement in the body, that is, they acquire a bodily habitus, to use Mauss's term. Yet, Noland claimed, there is a kind of kinaesthetic surplus that makes novelty possible: 'kinesthetic experience, produced by acts of embodied gesturing, places pressure on the conditioning a body receives, encouraging variations in performance that account for large innovations in cultural practice that cannot otherwise be explained' (Noland 2009, pp. 2–3). Dance movement, she concluded, is special because it is a realm of relative freedom. It is an appealing argument, and I suspect it persuades many contemporary dancers and followers of dance. There is a very evident investment by dancers in claiming agency for movement informed by subjective kinaesthesia and tacit proprioception. In spirit, the argument follows Mauss, who claimed that though all bodies, through movement and touching, acquire a socially specific set of habits, it does not follow that physiological or social forces completely dictate the possibilities of the subjective world and individual action.

As women had expressed earlier, when they took to the bicycle and when they removed the corset, freedom to move the individual body is also a social freedom. When Duncan freed the dancing body from the rules of ballet and turned to what she presented as the natural body, the body tuned to its breathing and illustrated in the arts of Ancient Greece, she exemplified the possibilities of agency. Generations of dancers subsequently have sought to be free to move and to feel movement as agency, and audiences have shared these feelings. This is as true in the many forms of popular dance in which participants 'let go' as it is for staged modern dance. All the same, if one considers public performance, and especially performance where a lot of people and a lot of money have a stake, one has to face questions about who or what has agency in which kinds of movement, the dancer or someone or something else. For the contemporary dancer, it is a pressing question: for whom does the dancer dance, and who owns and controls the space, or the medium, in which the dancing takes place? Yet, kinaesthetic awareness remains present as a confirmation of inner freedom.

This conclusion returns to the aphorism associated with Graham, 'movement never lies'. It is hard not hard to feel the force of this: direct, honest kinaesthetically aware movement contrasts with the duplicitous movements of gesture and speech so visible in the public sphere. Taken too literally, however, the saying is not true, since bodily symptoms expressed in posture and movement often enough create a wall of unconscious deception about what is going on. This is most clear in hysteria. 'Anna O.', to take the famous case, exhibited a paralysed arm which did not express an honest bodily condition but a psychological repression (in Freudian terms, an unconscious memory). A dancer may feel the back is straight, though the observing teacher may say it is bent. A person who has lost a limb may yet feel the limb move. Nevertheless, confidence in the body as a source of authenticity pervades performance culture. Performance culture is put forward as an ideal for political culture – as a microcosm for a projected political macrocosm – in which people present the body and its movements and appearances as the expressive medium of social truths and real or essential identity. Movement and what is said about movement in performance thereby engages with fashion and identity politics. The individual body and how it looks and moves becomes the site of political struggle. And, indeed, contemporary dance is a site for exploring relations between the body, movement, sex, race and gender: men dance in skirts, women lift men and women lift women, dancers wear identical costumes down-playing gender and movements and masks disown expression, race and sensuality. Dance radically questions conventional notions and asserts new identities.

There is, it scarcely needs to be said, much awareness of movement in sex. The mores of courtship and sexual relations turn around 'moves' made, 'moves' reciprocated and 'moves' resisted. Kinaesthesia is not usually central to a person's awareness of what is going on; yet is hard to conceive of sensuality without the presence of kinaesthetic sensibility. Because embodied, perhaps all forms of dance have some kind of connection with sensuality, even though this may be tightly contained (ballroom), kept at a distance (folk dance) or transformed into purified beauty (ballet). Questions of physical closeness and movement in relations between dancers, as between people generally, are often not sharply separable from questions about sensuous and erotic pleasure. How does the dancer respond in contact improvisation, designed to explore the unanticipated in movement, when barely concealed 'private parts' move close? How do actors while filming manage the passionate kiss, which Pablo Maurette described as 'haptic conversation' (Maurette 2018, p. 104)? When haptic technologies come online, will surface contact prove satisfying for sensual pleasure and calm the longing for physicality that we heard expressed during conditions of isolation?

The quandary, that Noland along with many researchers into the nature of scientific knowledge have considered, remains. Is it legitimate to refer to the body as an objective reality in principle describable in the same way for each person? This is the approach of the natural scientist. Or is anything asserted about the body already structured by social assumptions and is therefore in its nature a *text* created in a *context*? This has been an approach with significant impact in the humanities. Though I have not discussed this and put to one side the topic of realism, as a properly philosophical topic, it is relevant to note that the tenor of the discussion supports belief (*pace* Graham) that naive realism about bodily awareness is misplaced. A commitment to the presence of agency while moving and dancing, however, does not depend on naive realism but on awareness of the place of movement, of activity-resistance, in a person's life. Noland's belief that there is freedom to create new dance practice describes something real; and if we compare this creation with the situation of someone in a nine to five job or obeying orders in the police or army, it is very real indeed. We humans are embodied as flesh – who would doubt it? – but the variety of forms of movement, and the practices, rules and customs that govern movement, all of which we assess by comparison with other forms, gives flesh freedom in ways that make a difference.

Where there is freedom to move, there it is possible to attribute a form of agency. Everyday language simply reports feeling agency in movement, feeling to which kinaesthetic awareness contributes. Respect for each person as an embodied subject whose well-being depends on the capacity and freedom to move is therefore an underlying principle of liberal democracy. This, at least, is the ideal. Restrictions on freedom to move, on a large scale with controls on the migration of 'others' or with the arrest of people in political opposition or, less seriously but disturbingly, with lockdown during a pandemic, call the principle into question. Conversely, the cultivation of freedom to move for people who thereby are not 'others' but 'selves', people who pursue dance, sports, health, travel, political activism and a host of other movements, is political freedom. Giving or restoring mobility of parts of the body with prostheses or of whole bodies with vehicles vividly embodies the ideal. Movement in all its forms, if most vividly dance, is the clearest expression of what freedom means, either individually or collectively. Very significantly, the members of a dance troupe working together feel collective agency as they move; and when they improvise together, there is a feeling of shared open possibilities: 'we co-constitute and incorporate each other's experience' (Himberg et al. 2018, unpaginated).

Relations between people are replete with socially specific, culturally relative rules and customs about physical proximity, contact and movement. Commonly enough, women, for a range of reasons from caring for others (young children, an elderly parent), to social tradition, to physical ill-health or disability, stay at home or go out on closely defined paths. In these circumstances, they, or other women claiming to speak on their behalf, describe a restriction of agency. Even when there is freedom to move about in public spaces, women question the degree of agency there actually is for them to move in the way they want. Young black men in Western cities say the same. In many countries, there are police controls on the freedom of public movement. In Russia, for instance, buying a train ticket, let alone 'moving' residence, from one town to another, requires documentary evidence of identity in the form of an internal passport. With the COVID pandemic, this kind of over-seeing of freedom of movement spread in liberal democracies, with debate about whether it was necessary in order to give society as a whole agency in containing the virus. It confirmed the position of the issue of freedom of movement in politics which migration has long made central.

The general point need not be laboured. The feeling of movement matters socially, and all practice concerning agency, and movement as the expression of agency, is political in its nature. It is always possible to question the repertoire of 'moves' available to different people in different social situations. Many people in the performing arts embrace this conclusion. The kinaesthetic world is the sensuous partner of freedoms and oppressions.

12 Finale – con brio

It would be a poor conclusion that did not celebrate the sheer pleasure movement brings. The pleasure is intrinsic to awareness of *participation* in a world, awareness at once embodied, psychological, ethical and aesthetic. In a much cited lecture on dance, Paul Valéry declared that

> dance is an art derived from life itself, since it is nothing more nor less than the action of the whole human body; but an action transposed to a world, into a kind of space-time, which is no longer quite the same as that of everyday life. (Valéry 1964, p. 198)

His words introduced a performance by Antonia Mercé y Luque, 'La Argentina', who was central to the modern revival of Spanish dancing, dancing that glories in the sensory world of embodiment. But dancing expresses and sustains hopes for life that concern more than embodiment. I have argued that the hopes finding a voice in dance and in many other forms of movement centre on the joys of agency, that is, in a person participating as a force in a larger world of forces, as an individual power among social powers and as an expression of energy in a natural world of energy. Numerous dancers have expressed this desire for participation in religious or spiritual terms, and even as a means to transcend the limitations of embodiment. So close have dance and religion been thought to be that Kurt Sachs, in his classic survey of human dance worldwide, simply assumed that the sense of movement entered into the earliest foundations of the religious impulse (Sachs 1963). All the same, the dominant idiom of Western contemporary dance is secular. Its descriptive language, moreover, is often inward-looking, concentrated on dance's own traditions, techniques and practices. There are, perhaps, dancers who think they are concerned only with novel expansion of the repertoire of embodied movement. As this book has sought to show, however, there are other perspectives.

DOI: 10.4324/9781003368021-16

I have emphasized the movement *of persons*.

It is language associated with individualistic humanism, that is, belief in the individual human being as the focus of knowledge and the irreducible value setting the parameters of the life well lived. To this it may be objected that cutting-edge art, philosophy, techno-science and environmental thinking call humanism into question. The issues at stake are complex and folded in on each other. The relevant dimension, though, lies with the way the foregoing chapters highlight dancers (and artists exploring medicine and science, many sports people, climbers, therapists and other people) identifying the movement of material bodies as the most real, if not exclusively, 'real reality'. Movers and artists explore materiality in performance, and writers on what they do use the language of materiality, both to interrogate the body and to shock and displace the pretensions of established and, it is implied, elitist Western culture propagating some kind of immaterial culture. New work also explores imaginatively staggering new technologies – IT, biotechnologies and cyborg or mixed human-machine creations – which call traditional notions of the human into question. Art merges with speculative intellectual thought envisaging new, post-human life forms. Yet, this emphasis on materiality sits very

Figure 12.1 Hanging pair (2013). Photograph, Tomasz Jaworski. Courtesy of Tomasz Jaworski. Copyright © Tomasz Jaworski.

uncomfortably, and very probably inconsistently, with the assertion of radical egalitarianism, ideals of freedom of choice in life-style and ecologically aware consciousness. Where do these assertions and ideals come from and in what way could it be said that they embody material values or that values are in some ontological manner, that is in their actual nature, material? In performance, artists participate in argument about the values of social life and do not only present material relations. Similarly, in his 'philosophy of walking', Gros delved into what matters about walking and did not limit himself to describing its physicality (Gros 2014).

I see an art installation in the Moscow Museum of Modern Art. The artists, Luba Sautina and Rina Wolnykh, have meticulously and imaginatively displayed a variety of artefacts taken from daily life, playing with and turning upside down characteristic aspects of a girl's upbringing: sewing, fairy tales about where babies come from, the lore of herbal treatments, baking dough (Sautina and Wolnykh 2021). The art objects displayed are emphatically material; but the values explored, the imaginative images and the ardent commitment they articulate, are emphatically not. The values that question the material emblems of a girl's upbringing and inform the symbols, gestures and acts sustaining and questioning the values appear most obviously to grow from the roots and nourishment, the cultural capital, of a dismissed humanism and from discarded religious traditions. But, putting aside a polemic on such lines, I stress, rather, that in creating perspectives on kinaesthesia I refer to the living language of people living everyday lives. It is ordinary language, movement and practice, and certainly not only a supposedly elite humanism or supposedly discarded religious feeling, which talks about and shows concern for the feel of movement in life. Sautina's and Wolnykh's installation well showed this.

Discussion of the fact and of the ideal, or value, of participation through movement prompts a concluding thought. Perhaps it is untimely, in the sense in which Nietzsche described his early essays as 'untimely' because they went against the grain of contemporary intellectual preoccupations. Reference to embodiment is ubiquitous, and there is reason to link this with the advance of science, with critique of the legacy of European reason and with the out and out pressure to render all aspects of human life as purchasable commodities. Just how much embodiment has become central to modern culture and political economy may be gauged by a thought experiment, by trying to employ the word *ensouled* alongside the word embodied. The word ensouled is certainly not ubiquitous. After all, though, if the feeling for movement, informed by kinaesthesia, is central to the feeling of being alive, why should a person attribute the ground of that feeling to body and not to spirit? The question may at first reading look stupid, since the existence of matter, validated by natural science, but not the existence of spirit, is so widely taken for granted. The aspects of human experience put forward in this book, however, concern *the awareness* of movement, not the reality of matter or spirit.

The actuality discussed is a *phenomenon*, not a neural event, a process not stuff. The awareness is 'there'. The awareness, to be sure, correlates with neural events (though how, no one can say); but, the awareness consists of, or is formed through, qualitative differentiations, evaluations, for which a language of being ensouled, rather than embodied, might appear appropriate. In different times and places, such a language has certainly been used.

The point of describing human activity as ensouled would be to draw attention to, to sustain and to promote the values and purposes of activity. The description would ascribe value and purpose to the nature or identity of individual people and groups of people. Such

Figure 12.2 Movement of the child (2014). Photograph, Tomasz Jaworski. Courtesy of Tomasz Jaworski. Copyright © Tomasz Jaworski.

ascription, if not in the language of the soul, is pervasive in everyday life, not least in the commonplaces as well as profundities of the language of love. Art works, such as the installation with artefacts of a girl's upbringing, or dance displaying the liberated body, explore the facts of embodiment but also make declarations with non-material content. Even a choreographer whose stated purpose is the form of the moving body engages in a social process which values such purposes rather than some other objective, and this act of valuation, though embodied, is in itself not material. A climber on a rock-face is about as materially engaged as it is possible to be but is also fired up because the engagement is inescapably a matter of life and death (Lewis 2000). There is a need for a language with which to describe the ideals and purposes for which people move. The language of ensouled action might be appropriate for describing such ideals and purposes, even while there is no doubt that ideals and purposes are embodied.

It may appear obvious why the word ensouled is not much in use: modern culture, informed by materialist, scientific biology, is embarrassed by, when not downright contemptuous of, references to the soul as a relic of primitive, pre-scientific ages and societies. And it is surely right to think that biology and the neurosciences advance knowledge of a kind which could not possibly admit the notion of a soul. The form of understanding in these sciences excludes the notion. Yet, even hard-nosed scientists acknowledge, if only implicitly, that there are other forms of understanding than those in the natural sciences, since they assert the rightness, desirability, meaningfulness and even truth of their form of knowledge, and rightness, desirability, meaning and truth are not biological categories. Depending on the direction of argument of the writer, these categories have a social, rational, linguistic or spiritual nature – they derive from society, from reason, from language or from the activity of spirit. If, then, there are different forms of understanding, it is open to ask whether there are contexts and purposes for which reference to ensouled movement, alongside embodied movement, would make sense and be of value.

There are, indeed, naturalistic arguments in philosophy to the effect that it is possible to ground all social, rational, linguistic or spiritual assertions on propositions about biological nature. This, though, is very much contested, and if I put the arguments aside and take a position, it is plainly to do no more than to follow common practice in the humanities and social sciences. The book's outlook on the place of movement in life, on the values and meaning of embodied performance, support belief in the validity of forms of understanding which are not those of the natural sciences. They are, in effect, arguments through practice, through performance.

Significant modern uses of the word soul in English derive from the history of slavery and Caribbean and African-American cultures. References to soul music arouse no condemnation. In this setting, soul denotes something like the centre of the self, the centre which, belief maintains, cannot be bought or sold, though it can be lost or killed. It is the final reference point of individual identity. Importantly, in this usage knowledge of the soul comes through feeling not reason, and hence it speaks in music, dance or literature. Toni Morrison's novels, to take a notable instance, portrayed and legitimated reference to what she and many of her readers call soul, writing about the soul of people who themselves had been slaves or whose forebears were slaves and who thus knew what it was to be bought and sold but also knew what was not bought and sold. She wrote of the identity of black individuals in terms of the enduring presence of soul, assailed but self-preserving as a value, in the face of white political economy. The difficulty for many English-speakers in using the word soul in other contexts comes from conflating usage with reference to soul in Catholic and Orthodox Christian faith, in which the soul is a God-given miraculous entity. Modern scientists, when, as they occasionally have been tempted to do, write that they have empirically demonstrated that there is no soul, attack such belief, though, as I have said, there could be no place for belief in the soul in the form of knowledge of brain science. Interestingly, where the word for soul in languages other than English is in common use, as, for example, *dusha* is in Russian, this reflects an everyday willingness to suspend clear ontological commitment (in the form of statements about what stuff really exists) in order to refer to what matters and concerns feeling in a person's identity. In social worlds which use the language of soul, souls are present since individual people have worth, and the language of soul reports the phenomenal feeling and value of worth as a dimension of existence. And, to get to the concluding point, belief in worth is standard among people staunchly committed to the language and practice of embodiment, even though they disown reference to the soul. There appears to be a large contradiction. The living values of daily lives, which artists express in performance, are most certainly given embodied expression, but the language of embodiment cannot in itself adequately or fully describe what is going on. We need a wider understanding and richer language – which, indeed, we have 'to hand' in literature, artistic performance, the good walk, the joyful relationship, the valued ritual, the shared demonstration and, in a word, in movement.

The significant import of everything there has been to say about kinaesthesia and about phenomenal awareness of action-resistance is that there is no demand to choose between reference to embodied events or to ensouled events, to events attributed to body or attributed to soul (or mind). References to movement and action-resistance denote processes, relations and participations, not matter or spirit stuff. With this rejection of dualist categories, this 'movement' of the book reaches its concluding purpose, the inter-relation of perspectives on the kinaesthetic world.

People are participants in relations, and it is this participation which knowledge of action-resistance reveals and movement explores and expresses. Here is another passage from Shepherd's description of walking in the Cairngorms:

> The sustained rhythm of movement in a long climb has also its part in inducing the sense of physical well-being, and this cannot be captured by any mechanical mode of ascent... What! am I such a slave that unless my flesh feels buoyant I cannot be free? No, there is more in the lust for a mountain top than a perfect physiological adjustment. What more there is lies within the mountain. Something moves between me and it. Place and a mind may interpenetrate till the nature of both is altered. I cannot tell what this movement is except by recounting it. (Shepherd 2011, p. 8)

Not everyone will have or value such a poetic appreciation of the non-material forces in a relationship. But for everyone movement results in forming and changing relations. This is 'the dance of life'. In this dance, and in more precise and aesthetically challenging ways in dance performance, a person's movement takes part in the relations of movement that constitute the world.

Interestingly enough, my edition of Shepherd's *Living Mountain* has an afterword by Jeanette Winterson in which the English novelist used Shepherd's work to illuminate the value of writing and reading as 'a medium for the soul'. Winterson declared: 'You need not believe in the gods to believe in your own soul. It is that part of you that feels not obliged to materiality' (in Shepherd 2011, p. 115). Seeking to describe human experience of movement, there has been a good deal to say about embodied materiality and physicality of dancers, walkers and people in sports and daily life. But the discussion of embodiment includes, not excludes, the experiential feel of movement, of kinaesthesia and of action in relations. The importance of this to art, therapy and good living suggests it might be appropriate to speak about movement as ensouled as well as embodied. For Winterson, as very evidently for Shepherd 'in touch with' her mountain, 'imagination allows us to experience ourselves and our world as something that is relational and interdependent. Everything exists in relation to everything else' (in Shepherd 2011, p. 112). Just so. Kinaesthesia, among all the marvels of the senses, irreplaceably contributes to awareness of relations and interdependence.

The book set out to discern the value of kinaesthesia in everyday life and in the arts, to explore why kinaesthetic awareness in movement matters. This involved bringing psychological, philosophical and cultural perspectives into relation with each other rather than furthering any one speciality. As the book has been an exploration and not a scientific text, I conclude with an illustration.

A modest studio of musical movement takes part – participates – in a day to celebrate the work of Mikhail Matushin, a professional musician and amateur painter, a leader of the Russian avant-garde in the years of its flowering before and after the Revolution. There are talks, discussion and performances inside and in the garden of the house where he lived in the Petrogradsky district of Saint-Petersburg. The small wooden house is now the Museum of the Avant-Garde, while the garden at the back is grassed and shaded with fine old trees. The events are informal and modest, organized by and for the participants and a small audience. In 1913, Matushin and his friends explored experimental theatre. The artists, with Matushin composing the music, and with Kazimir Malevich doing the stage design, produced Velimir Khlebnikov's opera, 'Victory over the Sun'. They indulged a large element of futurist fantasy – humans take control of the life of the sun. In the garden, beside the grey tree-trunks, stand two-dimensional sculptures, or cut-outs, of peasants in Malevich's style. Over a century later, the group to which I belong (on this occasion, we are seven) joins others and rigs up speakers by the porch to the garden, and there we present much practised, though originally improvised, movements to the music. The sun is bright and comes dappled and blinking through the trees. We are not young dancers but we still move. We are barefoot on the ground, in contact with soil and grass. There is struggle in the music, conflict, but added to the unfinished piece is an ending taken from Scriabin, so that the dancers come together for a finale in a circle before and beneath the sun. The movement folds the past into the present and folds our present into what was a great moment of artistic innovation with hope for the future. The movement to the music establishes a relation, an embodied relation, and – why not say it? – an ensouled relation with past, present and future. The members of the group, collectively, are agents, enacting in movement actions which are emblematic of agency in daily life. There is power in what we do, not in what we impose on others. We gesture. We feel there is movement.

References and selected reading

*Marks selected sources with accessible overviews.

Alexander, Z. Ç. (2017). *Kinaesthetic Knowing: Aesthetics, Epistemology, Modern Design*. Chicago: University of Chicago Press.
*Andrews, K. (2020). *Wanderers: A History of Women Walking*. London: Reaktion Books.
Bachelard, G. (1964). *The Poetics of Space*, trans. M. Jolas. New York: Orion Press.
Bastian, H. C. (1880). *The Brain as an Organ of Mind*. London: Kegan Paul.
Bender, A. and Beller, S. (2016). Current perspectives on cognitive diversity. *Frontiers in Psychology* 7. DOI: 10.3389/fpsyg.2016.00509.
Bergson, H. (1913). *Time and Free Will: An Essay on the Immediate Data of Consciousness*, trans. F. L. Pogson. London: George Allen.
Bergson, H. (2004). *Matter and Memory*, trans. H. M. Paul and W. S. Palmer. Mineola, NY: Dover.
Bernstein, N. (1967). *The Co-ordination and Regulation of Movements*, trans. anon. Oxford: Pergamon Press.
Berthoz, A. (2000). *The Brain's Sense of Movement*, trans. G. Weiss. Cambridge, MA: Harvard University Press.
Berthoz, A. and Petit, J.-L. (2008). *The Physiology and Phenomenology of Action*, trans. C. Macann. Oxford: Oxford University Press.
Bible. (2008). *The Bible: Authorized King James Version*. Oxford: Oxford University Press.
Boddice, R. and Smith, M. (2020). *Emotion, Sense, Experience*. Cambridge: Cambridge University Press.
Bolens, G. (2012). *The Style of Gestures: Embodiment and Cognition in Literary Narrative*. Baltimore: Johns Hopkins University Press.
Brain, R. M. (2015). *The Pulse of Modernism: Physiological Aesthetics in Fin-de-siècle Europe*. Seattle: University of Washington Press.

Brandstetter, G. (2013). '"Listening": kinesthetic awareness in contemporary dance. In G. Brandstetter, G. Egert, and S. Zubarik, eds. *Touching and Being Touched: Kinesthesia in Dance and Movement*, pp. 163–179. Berlin: de Gruyter.

Brandstetter, G., Egert, G. and Zubarik, S., eds. (2013). *Touching and Being Touched: Kinesthesia in Dance and Movement*. Berlin: de Gruyter.

Canguilhem, G. (1994). Qu'est-ce que la psychologie? [What is psychology?] In *Études d'histoire et de philosophie des sciences*, 7th edn., pp. 365–381. Paris: J. Vrin.

*Carroll, N. and Moore, M. (2008). Feeling movement: music and dance. *Revue internationale de philosophie* 62: 413–435.

Chaiklin, S. (2019). The meaning and origin of the activity concept in Soviet psychology – with primary focus on A. N. Leontiev's approach. *Theory & Psychology* 29/1: 3–26.

Claid, E. (2021). *Falling through Dance and Life*. London: Bloomsbury.

Clarac, F., Massion, J. and Smith, A. M. (2009). Duchenne, Charcot and Babinski, three neurologists of La Salpêtrière and their contributions to concepts of the central organization of motor synergy. *Journal of Physiology – Paris* 103: 361–376. DOI: 10.1016/jphysparis.2009.09.001.

*Classen, C. (2012). *The Deepest Sense: A Cultural History of Touch*. Urbana: University of Illinois Press.

*Copeland, R. and Cohen, M., eds. (1983). *What Is Dance? Readings in Theory and Criticism*. Oxford: Oxford University Press.

Daly, A. (1992). Dance history and feminist theory: reconsidering Isadora Duncan and the male gaze. In L. Senelick, ed., *Gender in Performance: The Presentation of Difference in the Performing Arts*, pp. 239–259. Hanover, NH: Tufts University/University Presses of New England.

Dance Nation 2. (2020). At: https://www.youtube.com/watch?v=bJyqNqlxesw& feature=emb_logo (accessed Jan. 2021).

Dawson, M. (2014). Embodied and situated cognition. In L. Shapiro, ed., *The Routledge Handbook of Embodied Cognition*. At: https://www.routledgehand books.com/doi/10.4324/9781315775845.ch6 (accessed Jan. 2022).

Deleuze, G. and Guattari, F. (2004). *A Thousand Plateaus: Capitalism and Schizophrenia*, trans. B. Massumi. London: Continuum.

Derrida, J. (2005). *On Touching – Jean-Luc Nancy*, trans. C. Irizary. Stanford: Stanford University Press.

Desmond, J. C., ed. (1997). *Meaning in Motion: New Cultural Studies of Dance*. Durham, NC: Duke University Press.

Dewey, J. (2015). My pedagogic creed. In S. Totten, ed., *The Importance of Teaching Social Issues: Our Pedagogic Creeds*, pp. 223–231. New York: Routledge.

Dilthey, W. (2010). The origin of our belief in the reality of the external world and its justification, trans. M. Aue. In *Understanding the Human World. Selected Works,* vol. 2, pp. 8–87. Princeton, NJ: Princeton University Press.

Dutkiewicz, J. (2015). Pretzel logic: an embodied ethnography of a rock-climb. *Space and Culture* 18/1: 25–38.

Fingerhut, J. and Marienberg, S., eds. (2012). *Feelings of Being Alive*. Berlin: de Gruyter.

Foster, S. L. (2011). *Choreographing Empathy: Kinesthesia in Performance*. London: Routledge, 2011. At: http://danceworkbook.pcah.us/susan-foster/kinesthetic-empathies.html (accessed June 2020).

Foster, S. L. (2019). *Valuing Dance: Commodities and Gifts in Motion*. Oxford: Oxford University Press.

Franko, M. (1995). *Dancing Modernism/Performing Politics*. Bloomington: Indiana University Press.

*Fuchs, T. (2021). *In Defense of Being Human: Foundational Questions of an Embodied Anthropology*. Oxford: Oxford University Press.

Fuchs, T. and De Jaegher, H. (2009). Enactive intersubjectivity: participatory sense-making and mutual incorporation. *Phenomenological Cognitive Science* 8: 465–486.

Fuchs, T. and Koch, S. C. (2014). Embodied affectivity: on moving and being moved. *Frontiers in Psychology* 5. DOI: 10.3389/fpsyg.2014.00508.

Fulkerson, M. (2014). *The First Sense: A Philosophical Study of Human Touch*. Cambridge, MA: MIT Press.

Gallagher, S. (2005). *How the Body Shapes the Mind*. Oxford: Clarendon Press.

*Gallagher, S. (2014). Phenomenology and embodied cognition. In L. Shapiro, ed., *The Routledge Handbook of Embodied Cognition*. At: https://www.routledgehandbooks.com/doi/10.4324/9781315775845.ch1.

Gallagher, S. (2017). *Enactivist Interventions: Rethinking the Mind*. Oxford: Oxford University Press.

Gallagher, S. (2018). Theory, practice and performance. In E. Bryon, J. M. Bishop, D. McLaughlin and J. Kaufman, eds., *Embodied Cognition, Acting and Performance*, chapter 8. London: Routledge.

Gallagher, S. and Zahavi, D. (2021). *The Phenomenological Mind*, 3rd edn. Abingdon, Oxon.: Routledge.

*Gardner, H. (1993). *Frames of Mind: The Theory of Multiple Intelligences*, 2nd edn. London: Fontana Press.

Gibson, J. J. (1966). *The Senses Considered as Perceptual Systems*. Boston: Houghton Mifflin.

Gibson, J. J. (1979). *The Ecological Approach to Visual Perception*. Boston: Houghton Mifflin.

*Gilman, S. L. (2018). *Stand Up Straight! A History of Posture*. London: Reaktion Books.

Graham, M. (1992). *Blood Memory*. London: Macmillan.

*Gros, F. (2014). *A Philosophy of Walking*, trans. J. Hove. London: Verso.

Gurdjieff Dances. At: http://gurdjieff-dances.com/eng (accessed Dec. 2021).

Haley, B. (1978). *The Healthy Body and Victorian Culture*. Cambridge, MA: Harvard University Press.

Heidegger, M. (1967). *Being and Time*, trans. J. Macquarrie and E. Robinson. Oxford: Basil Blackwell.

Heller-Roazen, D. (2007). *The Inner Touch: Archaeology of a Sensation.* New York: Zone Books.

Himberg, T., Laroche, J., Bigé, R., Buchkowski, M. and Bachrach, A. (2018). Coordinated interpersonal behaviour in collective dance improvisation: the aesthetics of kinaesthetic togetherness. *Behavioral Sciences* 8/2. DOI: 10.3390/bs8020023.

Husserl, E. (1989). *Ideas Pertaining to a Pure Phenomenology and to a Phenomenological Philosophy. Second Book. Studies in the Phenomenology of Constitution. Collected Works*, vol. 2, trans. R. Rojcewicz and A. Schuwer. Dordrecht: Kluwer.

Husserl, E. (1997). *Thing and Space. Lectures of 1907. Collected Works*, vol. 8, trans. R. Rojcewicz. Dordrecht: Kluwer.

*Ingold, T. (2004). Culture on the ground: the world perceived through the feet. *Journal of Material Culture* 9/3: 315–340.

*Ingold, T. (2011). *Being Alive: Essays on Movement, Knowledge and Description.* London: Routledge.

James, W. (1950). *The Principles of Psychology.* New York: Dover.

James, W. (2000). A world of pure experience. In *Pragmatism and Other Writings*, pp. 314–336. New York: Penguin Books.

Jeannerod, M. (2006). *Motor Cognition: What Action Tells the Self.* Oxford: Oxford University Press.

Jonas, H. (1954). The nobility of sight: a study in the phenomenology of the senses. *Philosophy and Phenomenological Research* 14: 507–519.

*Josipovici, G. (1996). *Touch.* New York: Yale University Press.

Koch, S., Fuchs, T., Summa, M. and Müller, C., eds. (2012). *Body Memory, Metaphor and Movement.* Amsterdam: John Benjamins.

Kuriyama, S. (1999). *The Expressiveness of the Body: The Divergence of Greek and Chinese Medicine.* New York: Zone Books.

Lakoff, G. and Johnson, M. (2003). *Metaphors We Live by*, new edn. Chicago: University of Chicago Press.

Lannen, M. (2020). Per-forming the sense of touch: a spatio-temporal embodied technology of resistance. *Body, Space & Technology* 19/1: 22–55.

Lanzoni, S. (2018). *Empathy: A History.* New Haven, CT: Yale University Press.

Law, J. and Hassard, J., eds. (1999). *Actor Network Theory and After.* Oxford: Blackwell/*Sociological Review.*

Lem, S. (2013). *Summa Technologiae*, trans. J. Tylinska. Minneapolis: University of Minnesota Press.

Levin, D. M., ed. (1993). *Modernity and the Hegemony of Vision.* Berkeley: University of California Press.

Levinas, E. (1966). Meaning and sense. In A. T. Peperzak, S. Critchley and R. Bernasconi, eds., *Emmanuel Levinas: Basic Philosophical Writings*, pp. 33–64. Bloomington: Indiana University Press.

Levinas, E. (1998). Intentionality and sensation. In R. A. Cohen and M. B. Smith, eds. and trans., *Discovering Existence with Husserl*, pp. 135–150. Evanston, IL: Northwestern University Press.

Lewis, N. (2000). The climbing body, nature and the experience of modernity. *Body & Society* 6/3-4: 58–80.

Lloyd, G. E. R. (2012). *Being, Humanity, and Understanding: Studies in Ancient and Modern Societies*. Oxford: Oxford University Press.

Lloyd, G. E. R. (2021) *Expanding Horizons in the History of Science: The Comparative Approach*. Cambridge: Cambridge University Press.

Long, R. (2002). *Walking the Line*. London: Thames and Hudson.

Luria, A. R. (1973). *The Working Brain: An Introduction to Neuropsychology*, trans. B. Haigh. Harmondsworth, Middlesex: Penguin Books.

Macneill, P. U. (2014). *Ethics and the Arts*. Dordrecht: Springer, 2014. DOI: 10.1007/978-94-017-8816-8_13.

McNeill, D., Quaeghebeur, L. and Duncan, S. (2008). "The man who lost his body". In S. Gallagher and D. Schmicken, eds., *Handbook of Phenomenology and Cognitive Science*. Dordrecht: Springer. At: https://mcniellab.uchicago.edu/pdfs/IW_lost_body.pdf (accessed Dec. 2021).

Maine de Biran [M.-F.-P. Gonthier de Biran]. (1929). *The Influence of Habit on the Faculty of Thinking*, trans. M. D. Boehm. London: Baillière, Tyndall & Cox.

Makkreel, R. (2022). Diltheyan understanding and contextual orientation in the human sciences. In D. McCallum, ed., *The Palgrave Handbook of the History of Human Sciences*, vol. 1, pp. 109–131. Singapore: Palgrave Macmillan. DOI: 10.1007/978-981-16-7255-2_45.

Manning, E. (2009). *Relationscapes: Movement, Art, Philosophy*. Cambridge, MA: MIT Press.

Manning, S. (1997). The female dancer and the male gaze: feminist critique of early modern dance. In J. C. Desmond, ed., *Meaning in Motion: New Cultural Studies of Dance*, pp. 153–166. Durham, NC: Duke University Press.

Martin, J. (1936). *America Dancing: The Background and Personalities of the Modern Dance*. New York: Dodge Publishing.

Maurette, P. (2018). *The Forgotten Sense: Meditations on Touch*. Chicago: University of Chicago Press.

*Mauss, M. (1979). Body techniques. In *Sociology and Psychology: Essays*, pp. 95–123, trans. B. Brewster. London: Routledge & Kegan Paul.

Mayer, A. (2012). Gradiva's gait: tracing the figure of a walking woman. *Critical Inquiry* 38/3: 554–578.

Mayer, A. (2020). *The Science of Walking: Investigations into Locomotion in the Long Nineteenth Century*, trans. R. Blanton and T. Skowroneck. Chicago: University of Chicago Press.

Merleau-Ponty, M. (2002). *Phenomenology of Perception*, trans. C. Smith. London: Routledge.

Messner, R. (2014). *My Life at the Limit*, an interview by T. Hüetlin, trans. T. Carruthers. Seattle: Mountaineering Books.

Michotte, A. E. (1963). *The Perception of Causality*, trans. T. R. Miles and E. Miles. London: Methuen.

Montero, B. (2006). Proprioception as an aesthetic sense. *Journal of Aesthetics and Art Criticism* 64/2: 231–242.

Montero, B. (2016). *Thought in Action: Expertise and the Conscious Mind.* Oxford: Oxford University Press.

Morrison, K. A. (2009). Embodiment and modernity: Ruskin, Stephen, Merleau-Ponty, and the Alps. *Comparative Literature Studies* 46: 498–511.

Nietzsche, F. (1969a). *Thus Spake Zarathustra: A Book for Everyone and No One,* trans. R. J. Hollingdale. London: Penguin Books.

Nietzsche, F. (1969b). Ecce homo, trans. W. Kaufmann. In *On the Genealogy of Morals. Ecce Homo,* pp. 199–344. New York: Vintage Books.

Nietzsche, F. (2004). *Human, All Too Human,* trans. M. Faber and S. Lehman. London: Penguin Books.

Noë, A. (2004). *Action in Perception.* Cambridge, MA: MIT Press.

Noë, A. (2007). The critique of pure phenomenology. *Phenomenology and the Cognitive Sciences* 6/1-2: 231–245.

*Noë, A. (2009). *Out of Our Heads: Why You Are not Your Brain, and Other Lesson from the Biology of Consciousness.* New York: Hill and Wang.

Noland, C. (2009). *Agency and Embodiment: Performing Gestures/Producing Culture.* Cambridge, MA: Harvard University Press.

OED (2007). *Shorter Oxford English Dictionary,* 6th edn. Oxford: Oxford University Press.

*Parisi, D. P. (2018). *Archaeologies of Touch: Interfacing with Haptics from Electricity to Computing.* Minneapolis: University of Minnesota Press.

Pascal, B. (1995). *Pensées,* trans. A. J. Krailsheimer, revised edn. London: Penguin Books.

Paterson, M. (2021). *How We Became Sensorimotor: Movement, Measurement, Sensation.* Minneapolis: University of Minnesota Press.

Radman, Z., ed. (2012). *Knowing without Thinking: Mind, Action, Cognition, and the Phenomenon of the Background.* Basingstoke, Hampshire: Palgrave Macmillan.

Ratcliffe, M. (2012). What is touch? *Australasian Journal of Philosophy* 90: 413–432.

Reason, M. and Reynolds, D. (2010). Kinesthesia, empathy, and related pleasures: an inquiry into audience experiences of watching dance. *Dance Research Journal* 42/2: 49–75.

Reynolds, D. (1995). *Symbolist Aesthetics and Early Abstract Art: Sites of Imaginary Space.* Cambridge: Cambridge University Press.

Reynolds, D. (2007). *Rhythmic Subjects: Uses of Energy in the Dance of Mary Wigman, Martha Graham and Merce Cunningham.* Alton, Hampshire: Dance Books.

Reynolds, D. (2013). Empathy, contagion and affect: the role of kinesthesia in watching dance. In G. Brandstetter, G. Egert, and S. Zubarik, eds., *Touching and Being Touched: Kinesthesia in Dance and Movement,* pp. 211–231. Berlin: de Gruyter.

Rochat, P. (2001). *The Infant's World*. Cambridge, MA: Harvard University Press.

Rousseau, J.-J. (1996). *The Confessions*, trans. anon. Ware, Hertfordshire: Wordsworth Editions.

Rousseau, J.-J. (2014). *Reveries of the Solitary Walker*, trans. R. Goulbourne. Oxford: Oxford University Press.

Ruckmich, C. A. (1913). The role of kinaesthesis in the perception of rhythm. *American Journal of Psychology* 24: 305–359.

Rudneva, S. (2007). *Vospominaniya chastlivovo cheloveka* [Memoirs of a Happy Person]. Moskva: Izdatel'stvo Glavarkhiva Moskvi.

Sachs, K. (1963). *World History of the Dance*, trans. B. Schönberg. New York: W. W. Norton.

Sautina, L. and Wolnykh, R. (2021). Zvereboi. At https://mmoma.ru/en/exhibitions/gogolevsky/zveroboi_luba_sautina_rina_wolnykh/ (accessed Jan. 22).

Schechner, R. (2003). *Performance Theory*, 2nd revised edn. New York: Routledge.

*Schwartz, H. (1992). Torque: the new kinaesthetic of the twentieth century. In J. Crary and S. Kwinter, eds., *Incorporations*, pp. 71–126. New York: Zone Books.

Shapiro, L. (2011). *Embodied Cognition*. London: Routledge.

Sheets-Johnstone, M. (2011). *The Primacy of Movement*, 2nd edn. Amsterdam and Philadelphia: John Benjamins.

Sheets-Johnstone, M. (2012). Kinesthetic memory: further critical reflections and constructive analyses. In S. Koch, T. Fuchs, M. Summa and C. Müller, eds., *Body Memory, Metaphor and Movement*, pp. 43–72. Amsterdam: John Benjamins.

Shepherd, N. (2011). *The Living Mountain*. Edinburgh: Canongate.

Sherrington, C. S. (1961). *The Integrative Action of the Nervous System*, 2nd edn. New Haven, CT: Yale University Press.

Sidgwick, A. H. (1912). *Walking Essays*. London: Edward Arnold.

Sirotkina, I. (2021). Signs for a science: Aleksei Sidorov's choreology. *Studies in East-European Thought*. DOI: 10.1007/s11212-021-09428-z.

*Sirotkina, I. and Smith, R. (2017). *The Sixth Sense of the Avant-Garde: Dance, Kinaesthesia and the Arts in Revolutionary Russia*. London: Bloomsbury.

*Sklar, D. (1994). Can bodylore be brought to its senses? *Journal of American Folklore* 107 (no. 423): 9–22.

Smith, R. (2019a). *The Sense of Movement: An Intellectual History*. London: Process Press.

Smith, R. (2019b). The muscular sense in Russia: I. M. Sechenov and materialist realism. *Journal of the History of the Behavioral Sciences* 55: 5–20.

*Smith, R. (2020). Kinaesthesia and a feeling for relations. *Review of General Psychology* 24/4: 355–368. DOI: 10.1177/1089268020930193.

Smith, R. (2022). Human movement, kinesthesis, and dance. In W. Pickren, ed., *The Oxford Encyclopedia of the History of Modern Psychology*, vol. 3, pp. 1220–1243. Oxford: Oxford University Press.

*Starobinski, J. (2003). *Action and Reaction: The Life and Adventures of a Couple*, trans. S. Hawkes. New York: Zone Books.

Steinman, M. M. (2011). The kinesthetic citizen. Dance and critical art practices for Master of Public Art Studies. MA thesis, University of Southern California.

Stephen, L. (1936). *The Playground of Europe*. Oxford: Basil Blackwell.

Sterne, L. (1967). *The Life and Opinions of Tristram Shandy, Gentleman*. Harmondsworth, Middlesex: Penguin Books.

*Straus, E. W. (1952). The upright posture. *Psychiatric Quarterly* 26: 529–561.

Thompson, E. (2007). *Mind in Life: Biology, Phenomenology, and the Sciences of Mind*. Cambridge, MA: Belknap Press of Harvard University Press.

Tuthill, J. C. and Azim, E. (2018). Proprioception. *Current Biology* 28/5: 194–203. DOI: 10.1016/j.cub.2018.01.064.

Valéry, P. (1964). Philosophy of the dance. In *Aesthetics. Collected Works*, vol. 13, pp. 197–211, trans. R. Mannheim. London: Routledge & Kegan Paul.

Veder, R. (2013). Walking through Dumbarton Oaks: early twentieth-century bourgeois bodily techniques and kinesthetic theory of landscape. *Journal of the Society of Architectural Historians* 72: 5–27.

Veder, R. (2015). *The Living Line: Modern Art and the Economy of Energy*. Hanover, NY: Dartmouth College Press.

Volvey, A. (2012). Fieldwork. How to get in (to) touch: toward a haptic regime of knowledge in geography. In M. Paterson and M. Dodge, eds., *Touching Space, Placing Touch*, pp. 103–130. Farnham, Surrey: Ashgate.

Wade, N. J. (2003). The search for a sixth sense: the case for vestibular, muscle, and temperature senses. *Journal of the History of Neurosciences* 12: 175–202.

Walking-Artists Network. At: https://www.walkingartistsnetwork.org.

Wallace, A. D. (1993). *Walking, Literature and English Culture: The Origins and Uses of Peripatetic in the Nineteenth Century*. Oxford: Clarendon Press.

Wearden, J. (2016). *The Psychology of Time Perception*. London: Palgrave Macmillan.

Winnicott, D. W. (1958). *Collected Papers: Through Pediatrics to Psycho-Analysis*. London: Tavistock.

Young, I. M. (1980). Throwing like a girl: a phenomenology of feminine body comportment, motility, and spatiality. *Human Studies* 3: 137–156.

Index

Printed in the United States
by Baker & Taylor Publisher Services